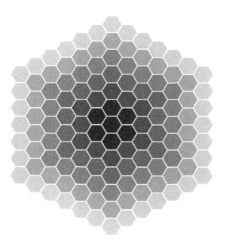

THE GIFT IS LISTENING

Enlightened
Relationship
Guide for Men

MysterE

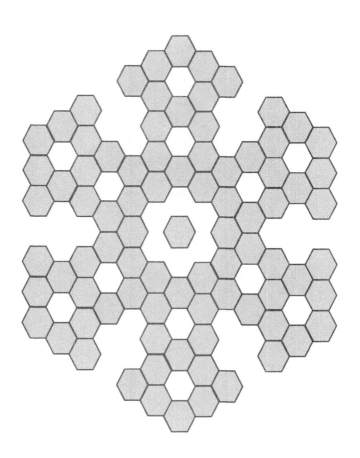

"The Gift is Listening"
Authored by: Mr E. Dan Smith, III
1/11/16
ISBN 978-0-692-61307-8

Published by: EaseUp, Life is Heart
@ The River House MysterE School
Boulder, CO 80305
www.lifeisheart.org

Cover Art: Dustin Brunson
Evolutionary Guidance: Kelly Moore
Proofreading: Ashley Lieber
Interior Graphics: MysterE
Book Design: MysterE
Editorial: MysterE
Content Source: 14

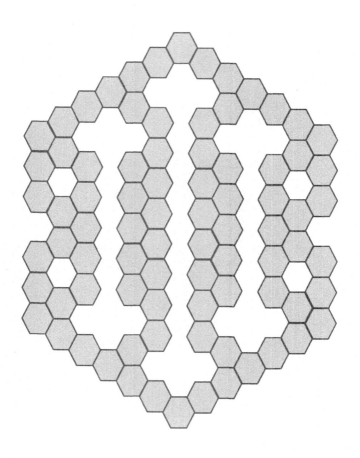

The Gift is Listening

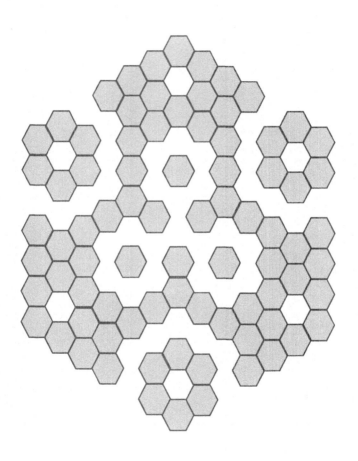

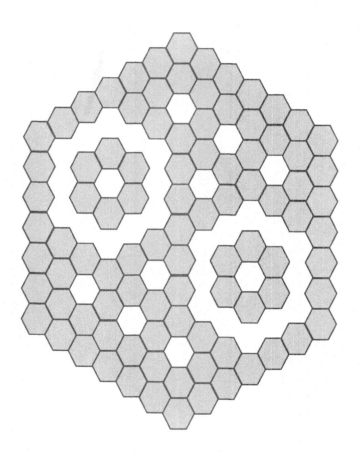

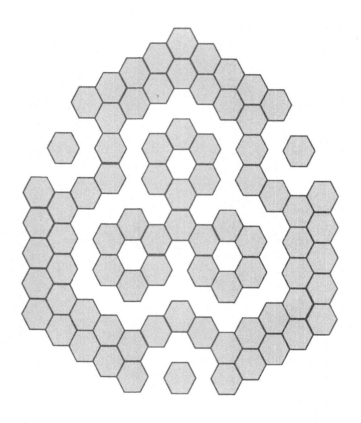

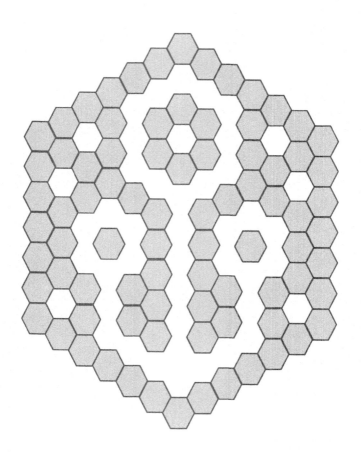

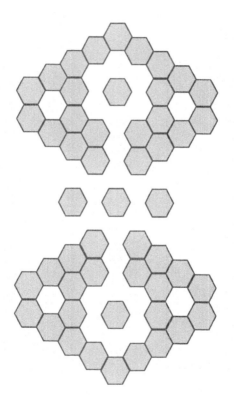

1 - An Invitation

Dear

Open-Hearted

Man

Only an Ascended Master waits for Now.
The human race cannot, and Now is now-here.
All the Ascended Masters have waited until Now.
When the polarity has reached an epic level.
When the environment is on the brink.
When the noise is louder than ever.
Now, listen to the Silence
For Now time is here.
Bring Christ to Your Heart.
And Bring Christ to Mother Earth.
Yes, this is the Second Coming of All Masters.
Christ is coming back as the Center of the Universe.
Align the Christ Center of the Universe with Your Center.
The Goddess is answering all prayers, Now, Be the One. Yes.

Absolutely,   *lovE*

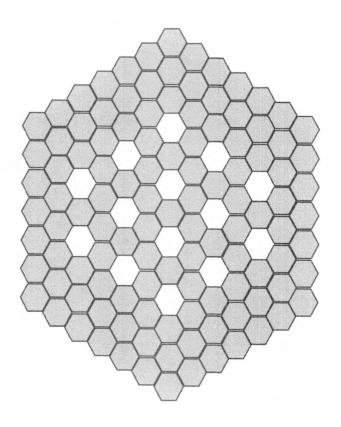

2 - Dedication

HEART LANGUAGE: Learn to Say... **Remember, instead of don't forget**... The Woman I Love, **instead of my girl friend / wife**. **The Mother of our Children, instead of my ex-wife**... **IAM going, instead of I have to go**... **IAM doing this, instead of She wants me to**... I feel that, **instead of I think**... **How is this a Gift, rather** than this sucks... **That Feels Right, instead of that makes sense**... I Imagine, rather **than I think**... **My Experience of You Is, rather than You are**... **I Feel the Impact of, rather than why did this happen?**... **How Was Your Evening, rather than who were You with**... **I Choose to Experience, rather than I need a miracle**... That is **Humbling, instead of what is wrong with me**... **IAM Feeling (anger), rather than You make me (angry)**... It Happened, **instead of She did it**... **This (Art) Challenges Me, rather than it's not good (art)**... **She Has Powerful Medicine, rather than She is a bitch**... **Everything is Happening Perfectly instead of I hope it works out**... **I have extraordinary Grace, instead of wow that was lucky**... **I would love to experience Her Essence, instead of I want Her**... **My Heart Desires, instead of I need**... **I would love to enjoy (Health), rather than I don't want to be (sick)**... **May I Share an Observation With You, instead of You need to**... **It Simply Is, rather than, that is wrong**... **That feels Like Truth, instead of that is right**... IAM Open to a New Way, rather **than that is impossible**... It is Happening, rather than it **is going to happen**... She is Free in Her Sexuality, rather **than She is a slut**... **I Did That to Wake My Self Up, rather than I am wrong or mistaken**... **I Forgive (Me or Her), rather than if only (She or I) had**... IAM Challenged by (Her), rather than **I don't like (Her)**... There is A Lot Going On and IAM Staying **in My Heart, rather than** I am overwhelmed... AND **most importantly, learn to say to Your Heart: "I require (love)" instead of I need, (love.)**

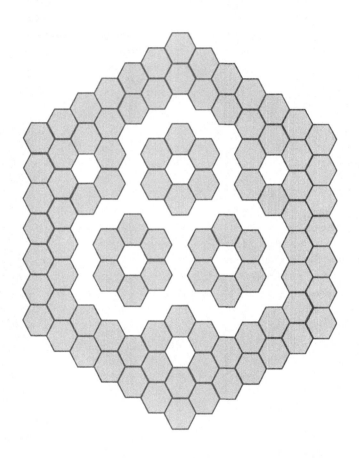

3 - Forward

One might imagine the author of this book to have a track record of enlightened relationship, or at least the credentials to back up his words. I have neither.
Qualified only
because my broken-open Heart has birthed a vision for the type of relationship that evolves humankind into the new paradigm.
A relationship
for all of time.
This 'twin flame experience" relationship is the basis for a collective shift in human consciousness. This book is simply an invitation for you.

I am committed to practicing this type of relationship to see what is possible. Therefore I extend my invitation: To live these musings and see where they take
Me, You & Us.
Are You ready for Love so pure, You attract a mirror of your soul, therefore becoming an active participant in human evolution?
Imagine and call
in a new destiny.
These 111 musings are coded to initiate a journey into the Heart for the pollination of an emergence for enlightening relationships for All.

The first time, read the entire book in order; opening your Heart to feeling and using your mind to imprint your consciousness with the shapes.
The more you read aloud, the more potent the magic.

Enjoy the musings and let go, so Goddess can bring what your Heart desires.

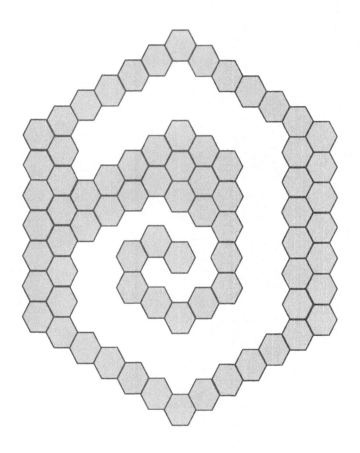

4 - Title

Who are you to deny giving One who makes your Heart sing anything? Do we not live in an infinite Universe in which all is provided for? Do you want to live in a state of joy and abundance? **Then** *give Her what She wants. And give it with joy. Isn't giving, the same as receiving? Then* **Gift** *Her what She wants by saying, "Yes, it's my pleasure." This opens the back of the Heart allowing you to receive more than you can imagine. If She was out late, celebrate Her fun with Her. If She falls in love, celebrate the new Love with Her. What She wants is to feel safe in Her expression. What She wants is for you to listen to Her. What She wants* **is** *for you to feel Her. What She wants is to feel alive. She won't rest however, until you learn* **Listening** *from the innocence of your Heart. If She wants freedoms, give them to Her. If She wants her own space, give it to Her. If She wants money from you, give it to Her. If She wants a release from you, grant Her wish. All you can do is give Her what you are ready to receive for yourself. But, what if She wants to fight? Then give Her something She cannot fight against. Invite Her beyond the madness. Allow Her to explore all desires. Desires of the Heart manifest great things. Desires of the shadow won't, but they do guide a person into their truth. And this is what scares you. From this point give Her what She really wants - which is Love. Love Her problem. Love Her struggle. Love Her craziness. Love Her addiction. Love Her challenge. If you give Her a fight, you are the One who is fighting. If you are fixing a problem you see in Her, you are the problem yourself. If you resist, you become the resistance. Let Her go into the journey of Her insecurities and Her desires while you feel deeply from innocence. When She feels safe in Her expression, your twin Hearts allow an initiation of purification. The old painful patterns and stories are swept up and burned away in your sacred union. Now you have given Her what She really wants. A Woman, in Her fullest creative expression is a Goddess who manifests anything She sets Her mind and Heart upon — and does so without condition. Her gifts emerge and are highly valued. She is always safe and provided for, and the community around Her is elevated. Which is why what you are wanting is irrelevant. What purpose do you serve by trying to get sex, or attention from Her, when you can receive so much more? Look at Mother Earth. When you give Her what She wants, how does She respond? When you fulfill your own desires first, what happens to the Earth? Then Give Her What She Wants. She's The Momma.*

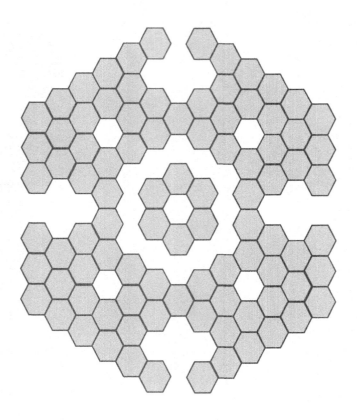

5 - How She Dances

The

poems are coded.

Every word has intention.

Some more than others for your Truth.

Be very open to allowing every message to be medicinal for you.

Resistance arising is part of the process.

It's your desire to know your Truth that takes you beyond limitation into the Compassionate Heart Consciousness.

Who can you partner with to stay committed through resistance?

For these poems change everything -

Allow Evolution to Guide.

Absolutely

Yes.

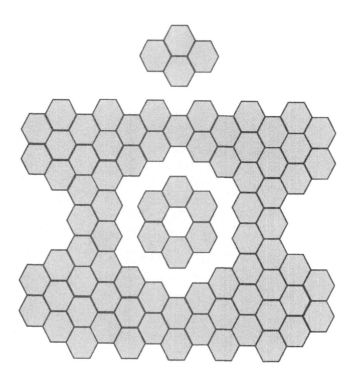

6 – Feminine Desire

Seeds

impregnate

the Earth's desire

to sustain life.

Earth

is nurture and nature for growth and abundance, naturally.

A man's seed impregnates the feminine desire to give and sustain life.

Woman is nurture and nature for the child, naturally.

When a woman feels something inside Her Heart,

a process of self-expression has been initiated.

She is pregnant with desire, naturally.

There is nothing you can do to stop this.

This is the most powerful source of energy known.

A woman may ignore or hide this feeling for some time.

However, Her Heart's desire is ultimately stronger than human will.

Unmet, Her desire is a disturbing force for shattering expectations.

So you might as well Give Her What She Wants right now.

You might as well align yourself with Her emergence.

Or She will quickly find a more willing partner.

7 – Advance Heart Language

Now,

slow way down.

You are passing on language from an older world.

The language you are using is not yours.

You are moving into the Light now.

You have everything to feed, clothe, & house everyone on Earth.

Slow way down,

Now.

What is Wanted?

What is wanted is to add the element of compassion to language.

Let's all speak from the Heart and

add compassion to our listening and speaking.

Adding compassion to language transmutes shame into Love.

Self-Compassion.

Yes.

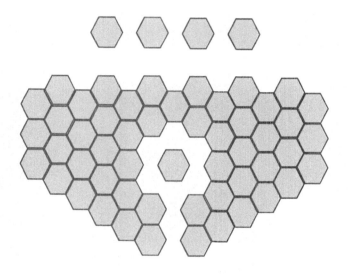

8 - In Every Woman

A Goddess Lives:

Whose energy is so pure that life comes to Her gracefully.

Whose sensuality is sacred, wild and transformative.

Whose Heart is centered in Divine Love for All.

Whose presence is calming and healing.

Whose life is purposeful and Light.

Whose reflection is crystal.

Whose Love is real.

Who is You.

Yes.

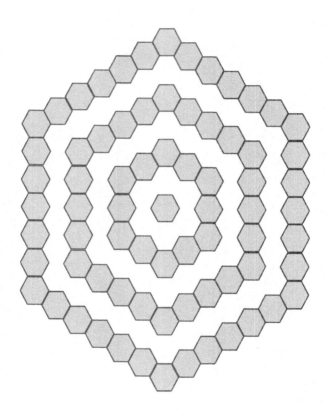

9 - Recipe

Yes,

Add Compassion

To the 3 Elements of Language

<u>*Tone*</u> *+ Compassion = An Open Heart*

<u>*Gesture*</u> *+ Compassion = Deep Listening*

<u>*Word*</u> *+ Compassion = A New Reality*

Linguistic Intelligence for All

Success is Love

Yes.

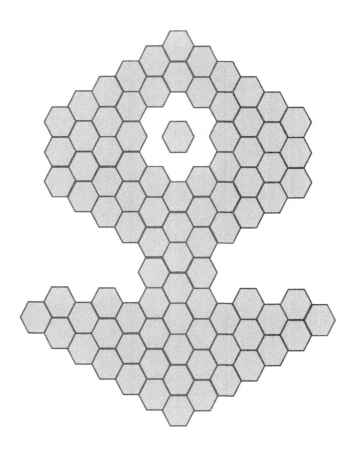

10 - An Open Heart

Re
member:
The purpose of
relationship is to heal.
This orientation prepares you
For what is coming. For time to time,
*an awakening **Goddess** takes Her lover to the*
*fire and **sets him ablaze**. She dispenses Her*
*medicine to **see** who is ready to accompany*
Her for the next leg of the journey. She
Looks for an Evolutionary Guide,
A man with authentic
Heart Presence.
You asked for this. You are the chosen One. Be that Man Now. Yes.
Take charge now by becoming responsible for Your own healing.
Open your Heart Presence by mastering Heart Language.
Be 100% responsible for ALL of Your life.
For ALL of Your feelings and actions.
And then, give up all control.
You aren't in control,
anyway, Silly.
Are You?

:-)

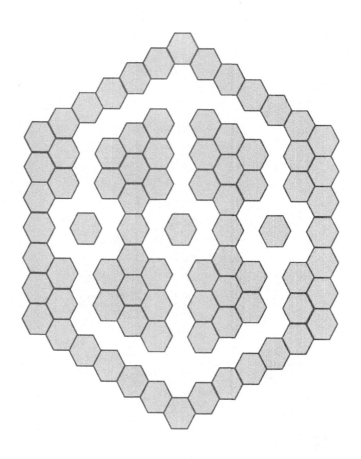

11 - Align Your Energy

Be
fore
You open
your mouth,
open your feeling body.
Align your posture vertically,
relaxed and attentive. Visualize your Heart
opening and become receptive. Breathe rhythmically
& deeply into the Center of
the Heart. Imagine Light
running from your Heart up
into the Heavens and down
into the Earth. Expand the
Light into a great bubble.
Look up, stretch your arms behind you. Breathe deeply.
Open to intuitive wisdom. Return to being
present with your life. Listen deeply
with all your Heart. Be new.
Repeat frequently.
Practice.
Yes.

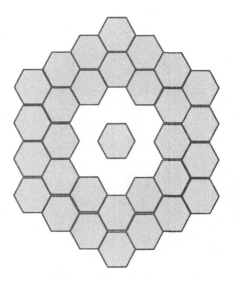

12 - Affirm

"Yes

IAM the Light.

IAM the Center of My Universe.

IAM the Creator of My Life Experience.

I bring my capacity to feel my Heart to Its fullness.

I summon Divine Assistance to Guide me,

To know my Authentic Self.

All is Provided For

Now."

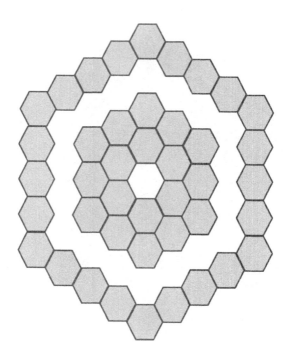

13 - Intend

"I AM

The Center

of My Universe, and

Honor Her as The Center

of The Universe. Our Hearts Align

for our mutual expression of empowerment.

From a clear Heart, I set My intent.

to follow the Absolute Yes.

Knowing All Is

Provided

For."

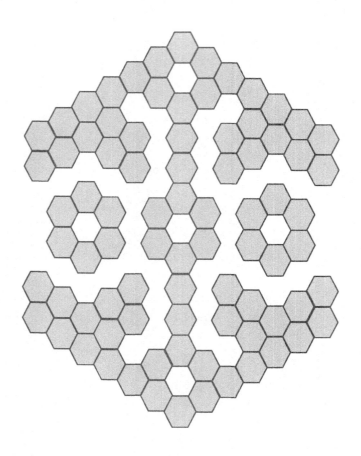

14 - Deep Listening

"Yes,

Universe.

I am the Center of You"

The ability to listen from an open Heart

is the alchemical formula that takes a woman safely

into Her feeling body in a way that is naturally transformative.

Seek Mastery in Deep Listening.

There many more ways to listen.

The power to heal through Deep Listening is the source of power.

When more hearts are synced up, more power is generated.

This evolutionary power ripples through humanity

from all the Centers of the Universe.

You are a Center of the

Universe.

Yes.

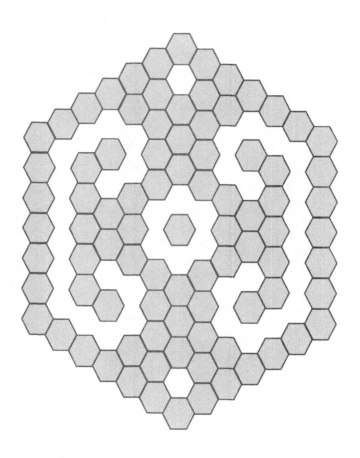

15 - Two Listeners

Now

There are two kinds of listeners:

Those who listen for evidence to support old limited storylines,

and those who listen innocently from Heart, knowing the story is never real,

&

the expression of feeling is paramount.

Which listener do you
intend to be
Now?

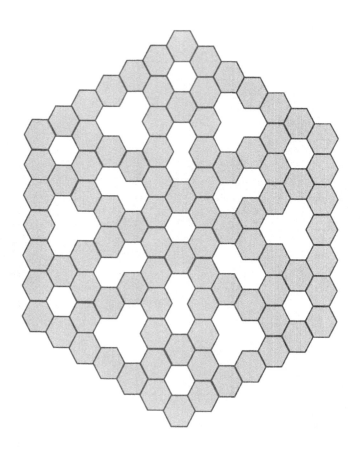

16 - Listen With Your Heart

When She is speaking, She reveals everything.
So orient from Innocence — of Knowing Nothing.
Trust your feelings to guide every interaction.
Speak only from the Heart's inspiration.

Justifying your position, is <u>not</u> giving Her what She wants.
Pausing to offer an empty space for Her to share is highly recommended.
Explaining why, is <u>not</u> giving Her what She wants.
Simple direct ownership of being a Divine creator is a good start.
Formulating a response, is <u>not</u> giving Her what She wants.
Sitting quietly and letting a new question emerge might be.
Reacting, or taking things personally, is <u>not</u> giving her what She wants.
Feeling Her Heart lands you back on solid ground.
Directing anger or finding wrong doing, is <u>not</u> giving Her what She wants.
Initiating forgiveness is always beneficial.
Discounting any of Her experience, is <u>not</u> giving Her what She wants.
Instead, inquire about how She feels.

When She is ready for you to share, She asks.
Answer directly from your Heart with vulnerability.
Own your Divine Feminine side — BE receptive to Her inquiry.
Allow your Heart to crack open and the tears to fall.

Then, receive Her.

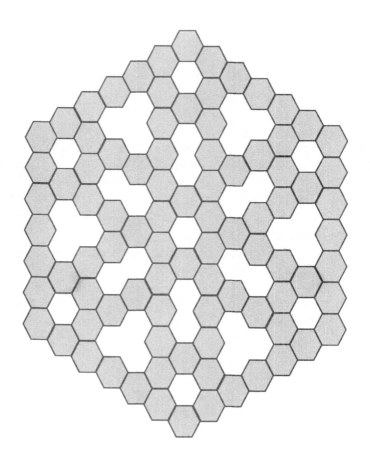

17 - Sing

"Om Hrim Anahata Guru Om"

Daily, or as much as possible -
Sing and chant this mantra with the tongue
rooted in the Heart to establish a field of Radical Trust.
This mantra is an essential element of establishing Heart Presence.

Translation:
Sanskrit:
Divine Mother, The Heart is my Guide, (or Teacher).
Spiritual:
IAM connected to the highest intelligence in the Universe.
Evolutionary:
All is Provided For Now.

(Ohmmm Hreem, Ah nah hah tah, Goo Roo, Ohmmm)

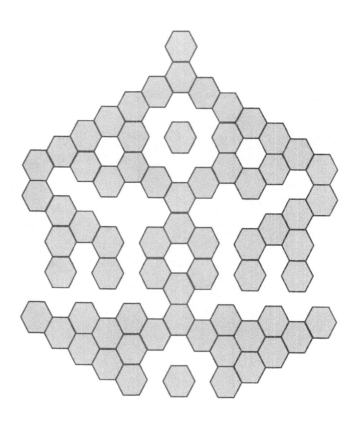

18 - Create

To

Use

Heart

Language

is to create sovereignty.

Use "I AM" to begin your statements.

Speak with feeling, from the Heart, in the present tense.

Bring old language into vertical alignment for empowerment.

When you originate from need, you bring limitation into the mix to source from others.

This horizontal

energy recycles and validates old stories and drama that disempower.

Humans in authentic power live beyond story to create a field of

Radical Trust with Linguistic Intelligence, opening space for

efficient healing, resource manifestation and joy.

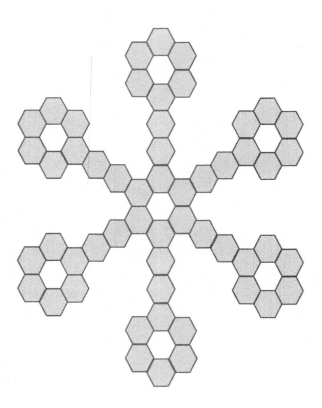

19 - A New Reality

In this emerging

era of We Consciousness,

humans are invited to refine the way

they make choices. Act only when you feel so much

harmony within your Heart that your mind is silent,

and resistance obliterated. Absolute Yes is

a tremendously powerful

flow of energy.

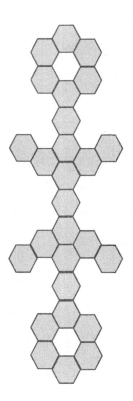

20 - The Mirror

"*Yes,*

I Give to me,

When I Give to Her.

What I see in Her, I see in me.

She is a perfect mirror of Divine Love.

When my presence produces harmony, I AM aligned.

When my presence reveals static, it's time to look within to heal.

When my presence reveals static, it's time to look within to heal.

When my presence produces harmony, I AM aligned.

Likewise, all of life is a mirror of Divine Love.

What I see in Life, I see in me.

When I Give to Life,

I Give to me,

Yes."

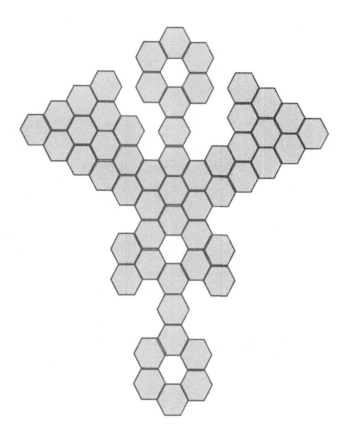

21 - 100% Responsibility:

A man responsible for his life and healing, lives in a paradox:
He is powerfully in charge of his intent and energy, owning & creating
100% of his life experiences, yet he recognizes he is in 0% control.

She will sing from Her Heart when She feels safe enough.
You have the capacity to open to that place for another.

First, master the Heart Presence in Your Self.
Open beyond your limited perspective.

An instant feel and it's gone.
A healing happens.

Absolute
Yes

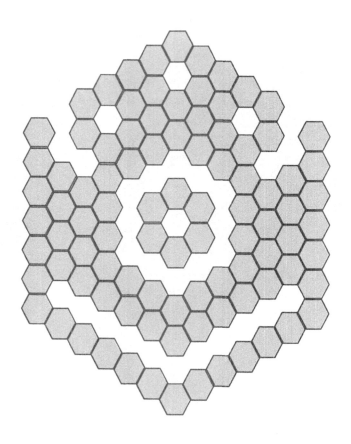

22 - Absolute Yes

A   big
river   of Light
  flowing in and out   and through all
    things and people, connected   to Divine Love & directed by
      Heart Language. Absolute Yes is   the result of transparency and
        using the Heart Language to exhibit Self-compassion & authentic
          expression. Only clear and empowering Choiceless Choices
              present - always providing adventures of safety,
                  peace, fun, serendipity, abundance and
                      e x p a n s i v e   l o v e.
                          y   E   s

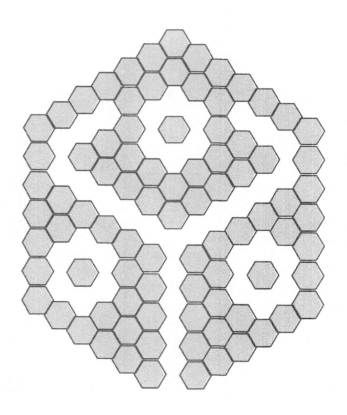

23 - Heart Presence:

Healing happens purely by Heart Presence.
When two Hearts come together in an Absolute Yes,
Trust becomes the looking glass into new human reality.
Love is but the merging of the new consciousness with the old.

You are offering the gift of the element of compassion to Her.
If She remains joyful, Give Her more of What She Wants.
If drama enters the field, step back and create space.
Investigate with feeling as to what is happening.
"IAM not in control of what is happening,
but I must now be responsible."
"What is my
relationship
to the drama?"
Stay in Heart Presence.
Stay above the drama unfolding.
Let Her fall into the empty space of Her tears.
Manifest Truth through courageous exploration of emptiness.
The man holding the mirror allowing Her to purify is also purified.

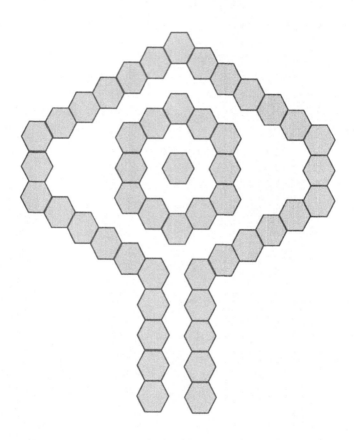

24 - Giving It To Her

Neither wanting nor needing anything in return, Say to your beloved:
"If it is in my power to give it to you, I gift through Divine Love.
I give it to you now with pure blessings of empowerment.
I am investing in your joy, Light and well-being."
All human beings desire to be met in Love.
Now, Give Her What She Wants;
do it completely with Love.
In the Absolute Yes.
You gift Her.
Always.
Yes
Yes
Yes
Yes
Yes
Thank you. Thank you. Thank you.

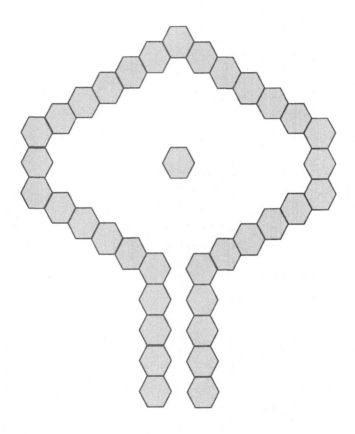

25 - Not Giving To Her

When you give Her what She wants and it no longer feels right,
What is the next step?
Ask your Heart for a clear sign to know the Truth.
Then follow intuitive guidance.
The Universe is transparent and answers directly to Heart's inquiry.
This request is always answered in reflection.
If you cannot give to Her with Love, You cannot give to Her freely.
You are in judgment or fear, or you have been enlightened
that what She wants is poisonous.
Either way it is no longer an Absolute Yes.
Now become devoted to Give Her what She Really Wants.
From here invite Her to into your Heart Presence.
Meet Her there and See Her Goddess.

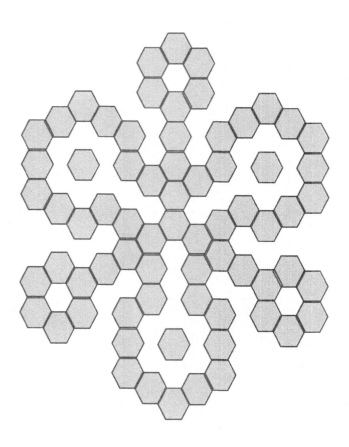

26 - Contrast

Oops,

Life Happens.

"This isn't what I asked for!"

Or perhaps it is?

Yes

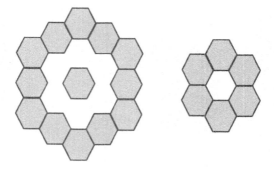

27 - Purpose Of Love

One
Currency:
Love in the form
of a twin - faced coin.

One side is the reflection of Pure Love.
Let the attraction pull you in to amplify Love.

The other side of the coin is the reflection of your healing.
Use the mirror to transmute your emotional pain into more Love.

Love is calling you to create more Love by resolving what appears as 'not love.'

When in Love see & feel the perfection.
When not in love, feel to see the perfection.

In You   in Life.

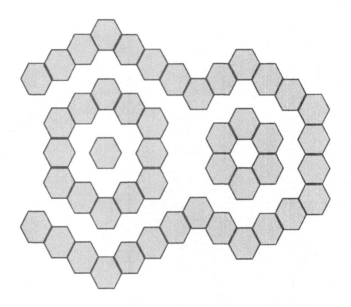

28 - Relationship Change

To heal is
the purpose of every relationship.

So,

When the healing wants to happen, the attraction field shifts.
Therefore, the relationship shifts.
It's not personal — it's energetically evolutional.
If your partner is required to be the mirror for your continued awakening,
then your mutual attraction state reflects that Truth.
If the attraction wanes, let your Heart Guide.

Trust that.

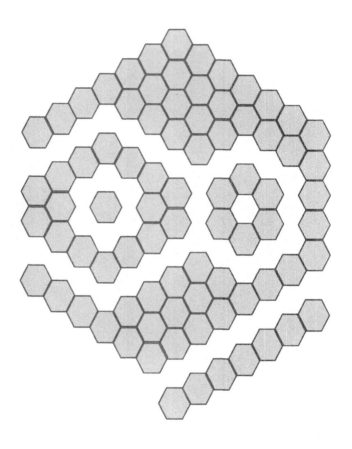

29 - She Ends It

She

may prefer

a gun in Her mouth

over a spoonful of honey. It's

just the way for Her, for now.

You may do everything right.

And still, She's not receptive.

She requires more contrast.

Allow Her to go. Don't

ask why She left

you.

Grieve instead.

Accept you are no longer a vibrational match.

There is no evolutionary learning at play except to Love

Her Divinely. Speak of Her beautifully to honor your connection.

You know not what Her soul requires for awakening.

So, stop trying to get Her back, and

begin a new relationship.

With your

Self.

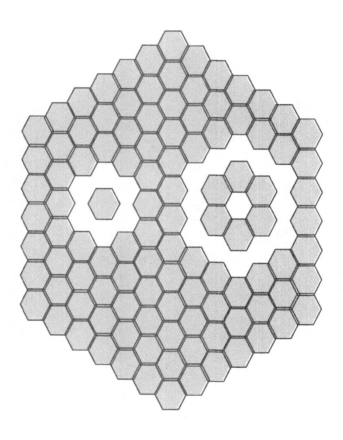

30 - You End It

When She isn't ready for healing.
She stops listening and focuses on what is wrong.

When your Heart Presence no longer provides transformation,
there is nothing to change,
There is nothing to fix.

It is time for some space.
Stay true to your Heart, and Love Her.
From an honorable distance.

When and if She is ready to re-engage, She lets you know.
In the meantime, keep your pants on.

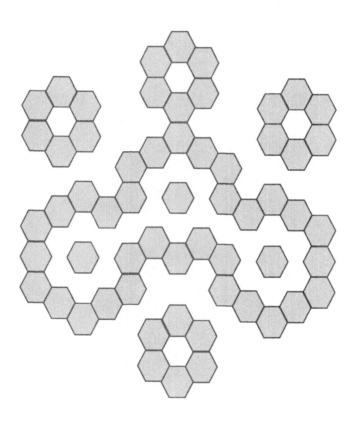

31 - Jealousy

Jealousy

arising has two paths.

One unchecked path leads to energy loss, and destruction of relationship.
The other path is an immediate opportunity for transparency and vulnerability

to ReFrame perspective for immediate healing.

Male shame would be to try to keep Her from another.
Find a Way to freely Give Her What She Wants,
Let Her discover the truth of Her desire.
So She feels free to taste it, or not.
She may be back, or not.
Radically Trust.
Heart.

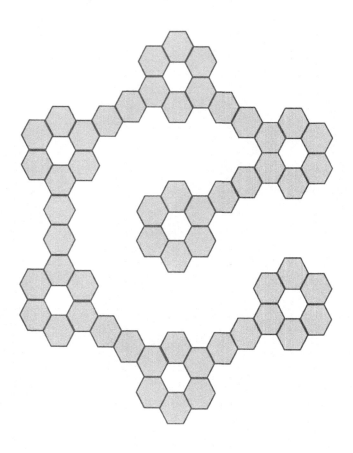

32 - Failure

There is no failure.
Don't even speak of it.
It is contrast for your evolutionary learning.
What you imagine to be moral failure is a mind-oriented self-judgment, which has roots in your shame.
Your ego is cleverly protecting itself by causing you to imagine wrong doing when there is none.
Needing to forgive yourself for perceived sins is out of alignment.
Forgive feeling instead.
Simply arrest your thinking to go beyond story, and internally investigate
the energy holding story.

Then practice forgiveness with feeling.

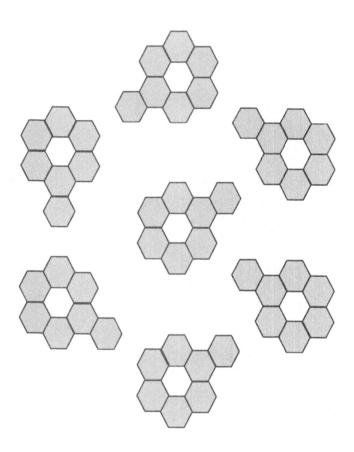

33 - Lying

When someone is untruthful, uncertainty about
everything comes into question and the trust field is broken.

Rather than building a case or confronting Her with your suspicion,
open your Heart and ask for the Truth to be revealed.

Then Love Her completely and fully,
trusting in Divine Perfection
so all Truths are shown
naturally in Divine
serendipity.

Then step into a new Truth, and spiral up together.

Or not.

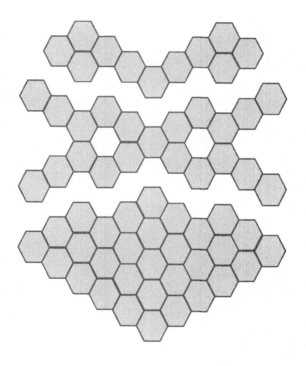

34 - Betrayal

There is no   such thing.
What is the Truth that you have betrayed your Self from realizing?
It's shame wearing a mask. She simply didn't feel safe enough to relate
Her Truth. What is the Truth you have betrayed your Self from realizing now?
There is no such thing. It's   shame wearing a mask.   She simply
didn't feel safe enough   to relate Her Truth.   What is the
the Truth you have betrayed yourself from realizing now? There is no such
thing. It's shame wearing a mask. It's shame wearing a mask. It's
shame wearing a mask. It's   shame wearing a mask.

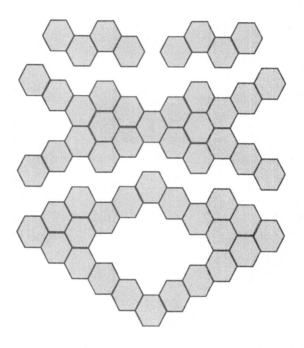

35 - Anger:

Men have been skillful at directing their anger to create.
They have created safety but not safe community.
The Goddess has willingly come along.
But for not much longer.

Your anger is your anger.
Feel your anger when She wants more and more.
Feel your anger when your 'needs' are not met.
Be courageous and say:

"I am angry and my mind is making up a story (that you are the cause)."

Open your Heart to transform anger into Love.
It is more fun to create by directing Love.
More is created — all from an inclusive place.

Set Her free, and then free yourself from your anger.
Use your anger for dissolution of illusion,
rather than for destruction of the Goddess.

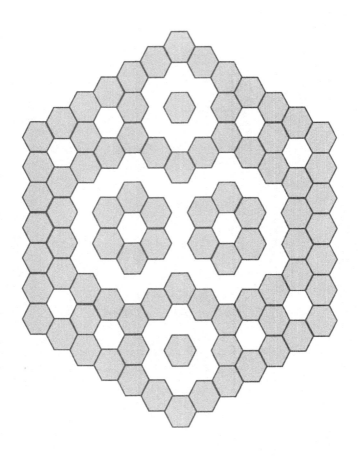

36 - Urges Of Addiction

Urges of addiction are
a signal of the next awakening.
Denying urges denies your awakening.
Go into your emotional suffering with Love.
It may not happen the first time, or the second.
You must keep going.   Even if it takes you to your
knees and then far beyond into your inability to arrest
the spiritual cleansing by your hand.   At this point, the
magic begins spinning. It is this alchemy that uses the raw
materials of your shame and pain to spiral you into a new
place of empowerment and joy. We each can create a new
energy source for our evolution, for ourselves and others.
This is the new conscious energy industry that evolves
humanity. It is more than sustainability. This is
evolutionary. To make evolutionary strides
as humanity - it is **our** *highest call of*
service then to each individually go
beyond our addictions, emotional
pain
and suffering into and through
the passage of the Heart. Then
we are ready to Guide others.

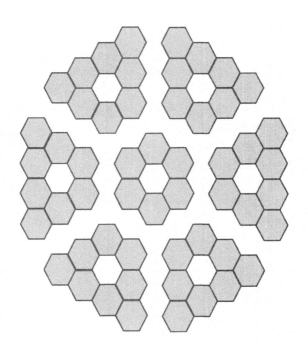

37 - Sabotage

Waking up

is going through your addictions without shame.

Practice forgiveness as you slip and fall to resurrect your Self with joy.

The potency of your personal intent is the channel that takes
you to the places you have protected your Self from.

Your Open Heart and commitment to forgiveness
is how to make safe passage to the other side of your outdated reality into
a new Open-Heart Consciousness.
From here all potential is realized, and all dreams become reality.
Evolutionary Learning,
remember? Yes,
You do.

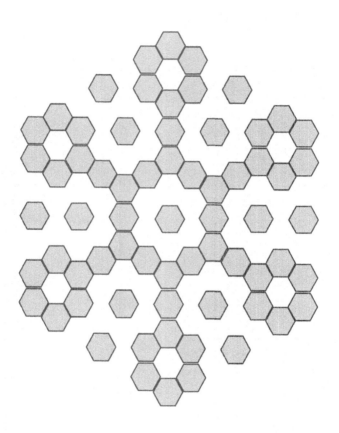

38 - Fantasy

Now Here.
This is the Test.
This is the Universe.
This is the Planet.

You cannot escape the challenges of this reality,

but you may utilize fantasy as temporary salve.

However, what is made in mind,
must come tumbling down.

So, to what are you saying yes?
Are your hands in the dream of your life?
Or have you misplaced your will in a mirage?

Listen to the Heart and BE transparent in your activity.
Clarity is the playing field in which the play of life presents itself.
Surrender the character roles of the shadow for an illumination of truth.

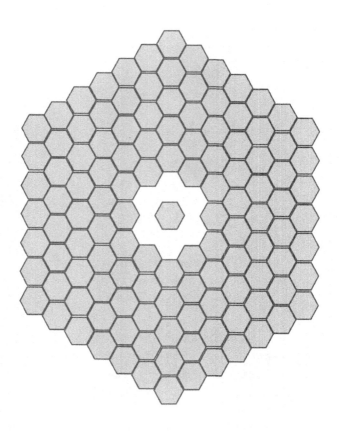

39 - Getting Stuck

It is time to Listen with all your Heart.
Feel deeply inside of everything.
Open your Heart to all feeling.
Free yourself of reactive decisions and obvious choices.
There is always another option.
When there is confusion in your mind.
When you don't know which door to take.
When the options are clearly in front of you, but there is hesitation. It's a
(PAUSE)
signal to stop trying to figure out the best option and sit quietly with the
energy running between the poles of choice.
Your mind doesn't need more information.
Your mind needs to get out of the way.
From a place of silence, bring a sense of neutrality to your mind by
opening the Heart to feeling.
Feel deeply inside of everything.
It is time to Listen with all your Heart.

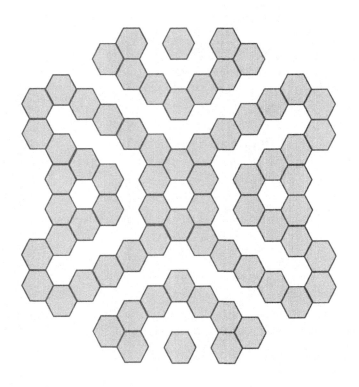

40 - Addiction

T

h

e

r

e

i s

n o-

t h

i n g

wrong with (pornography.)
It's your relationship with
it. Everyone is addicted
to something. You are
not addicted to (porn.) You are addicted to shame. Your sexuality is a
great power. Use discernment where you direct this energy. Less become the
object of your
obsession.

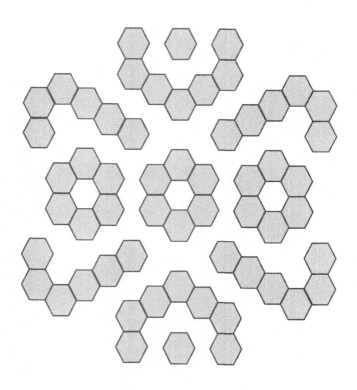

41 - Drama

*Drama is
an addiction
of spinning stories
to hide feelings and justify
circumstance.*

Refuse to participate.

*Drama is a signal of a coming awakening - and an invitation for you
to be a partner in the transmutation of the feeling causing the drama.*

*Drama is the indicator
for Deep Listening, with
yourself first, and then with Her.
When the drama remains in Her,
and you are in Heart Presence.
Take your Heart Presence someplace else.*

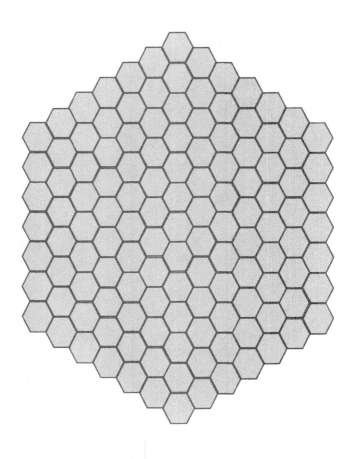

42 - Health

It is

impossible to get disease when the body is clear of shame.

Success

is just as

unhealthy

as is failure.

Both are poles.

Polarity is not healthy.

But is primed for awakening.

What addiction is masking your emotional healing?

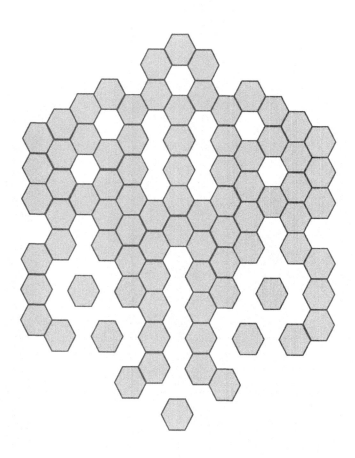

43 - Addiction Mirror

The spiritual
key to transforming addiction
is to find the mirror image of the addiction
itself in one primary relationship in your life. There is
one relationship in every awakening person that
mirrors the energetic pattern of the addiction cycle
they wish to transform. When you attempt to heal an
addiction by itself, you are in polarity with (against)
your addiction. There is an opportunity to heal the
addiction and shift the relationship at the same time.
Although it appears that meeting two challenges at
once would be harder, it works exactly in the opposite
way. Removing yourself from polarity, allows you to
see the entire mosaic, and therefore the Truth. By
being willing to be open to the addiction cycle and the
disempowering relationship together, you go more
quickly and with greater power to the source of both
(which is the same.) By loving and appreciating the
denser energies of both situations, you create a shift of
perspective for healing by adding compassion. Oh yes.
This creates an evolutionary fusion - when the energies
consume another. A radical allowance bringing
in Light and energy for rapid
transformation.

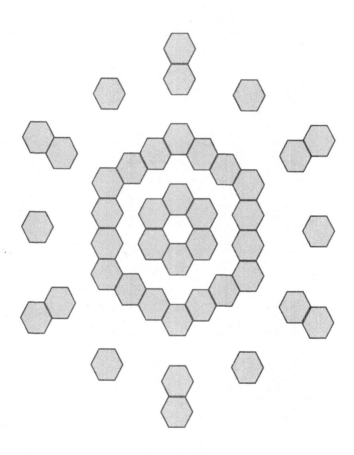

44 - Courage

There is no reason to wait.
Dive into the vastness of feeling within.
It's your courage to sail into the river that creates a wake behind you.
Becoming a wave of wakefulness raising all boats in the river.
But you have to get in the river first.
Learn to ride the waves with joy.

Come on my Heart friends.
The water's cold and icy at times.
But sometimes it becomes a warm lake.
Other times moving like the Colorado rapids.

But it is safe to journey.

Where we are going is Perfectly Perfect.

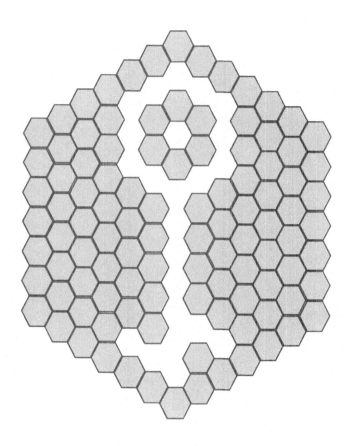

45 - Owning It

"Yes,
I did this-
All of it."

"I placed myself in life exactly as I am.
I AM responsible for everything I AM experiencing.
I have the free will choice to powerfully create my reality."

Speak your Truth.
Own your darker side.
Come clean on your secrets.
Communicate your 'needs' to others.
Create negative space inside with forgiveness.
Your mission is to fully reveal yourself in Radical Trust.
Increase your manifesting power by using the Heart Language.
The human constellation cares for everything when you are transparent.
A compassionate action: allow dramatic relationships to naturally fade away.

You are meeting new Brothers and Sisters for a reason.
These relationships are far more potent in Heart Presence.
Clean it up with your ex-lovers so a harmonic field exists for All.

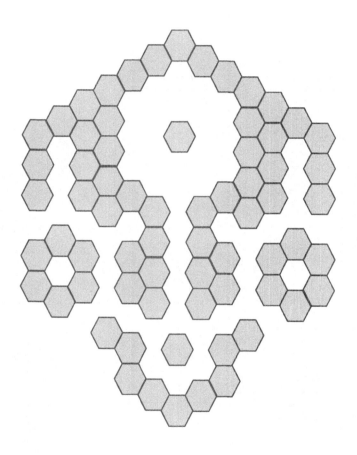

46 - Transmute Suffering

Let your feelings guide you

through the turbulent waters into the still pond.

Hone your recognition of Truth in the chaotic wild.

Find the lion tamer of the shadow.

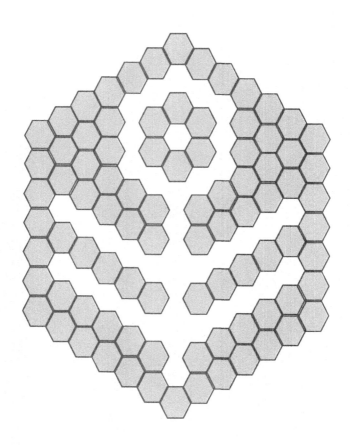

47 - Be Alone Single Man

Be Radical
Honor Human Sexual Intimacy.

Be Patient
Refine your attraction state to meet people in a new way.

Be With Your Self
Love yourself and others without your penis' involvement.

Be Curious
Observe your mind pulling you toward addiction.

Be with Desire
Every time you feel the urges,
open your Heart instead.
Expand Your Power
For discernment
creation
now.

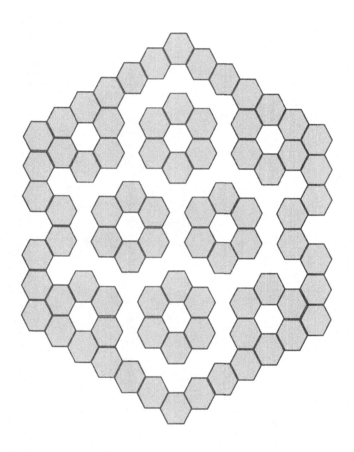

48 – Discernment

An efficient utilization of energy.

*Knowing between difference between Heart's desire
and the desires of the unconscious.*

Say Yes to everything in life.

Engaging only when the Absolute Yes is present.

Especially in intimate relationships.

Engage with expansive energy.
Keep your pants on.
Be weightless.
until its

tim

e

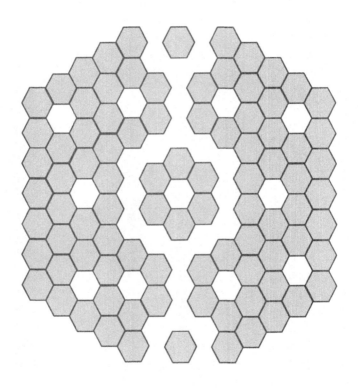

49 - Create Space

In every Human Heart is the entire cosmos.
To find the hidden door, create space
by expanding your awareness.
There is a Tiny Space
inside your
Heart.
Patience for
the Absolute Yes
Brings old pain to you.
Ask the Tiny Space to activate.
N o W
Simultaneously draw your shame into the Space.
N o W
Breathe in and out of the Tiny Space.
Focus your will on centering
your awareness in the
Tiny Space.
Ask
for help
in expanding
the Light of the Heart
into the Light of the Universe.
Be willing to feel everything and let go.

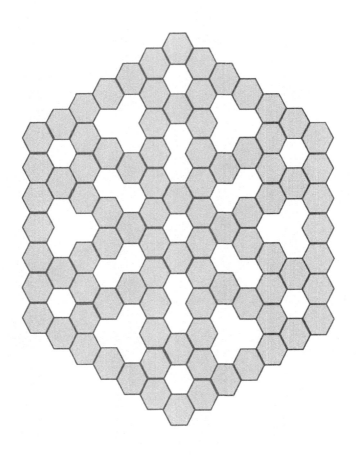

50 - Morality

Now,
there is no right and no wrong.

There is:
an efficient use of energy;
An expansion of your vibration
leading to enlightenment,
gracefully now.

OR

There is an
inefficient use of energy;
A contraction of your vibration
leading to enlightenment,
karmically now.

You choose Heaven or Hell in every
Now.

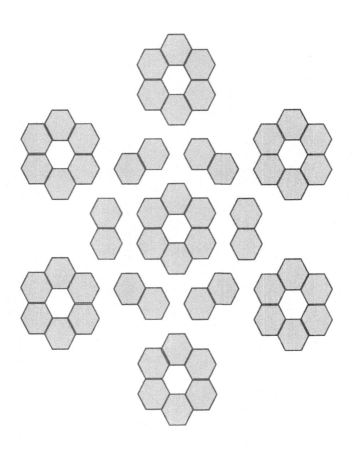

51 - Trust

The illusion is that you need to trust Her.
Trust your Heart instead.

The Trust Field is important.
Vital to what's happening.
But it comes from you.

Trust is revealing your Self so completely,
There is nothing left in the way of receiving.

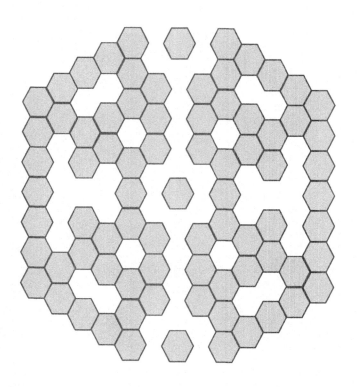

52 - Goddess Medicine

When words tumble

from Her mouth

that activate you

emotionally, they

represent medicine for you. When you are triggered by Her,

it is a reflection of your pain. She is providing a pure mirror

for your healing. To make your suffering Hers - is to be in

resistance to Her med-

icine. And therefore

the Divine Goddess.

Take your Medicine,

A

b

s

o

l

u

t

e

l

y

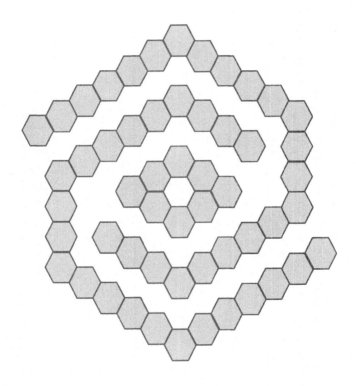

53 - Goddess Wrath

It   is

not   foul .

Find Love for the Goddess

hiding **beh**ind Her **pro**jections.

She is like a great feline, growling

and showing off Her teeth. She is

merely testing **HER** environment.

Is it safe to emerge

with my gifts?

Your acknowledgment of the

alchemy at hand channels rays of

Light through your Hearts. Fear is

swept away in a river of Light

knowing

one part

of God

cannot

harm

another.

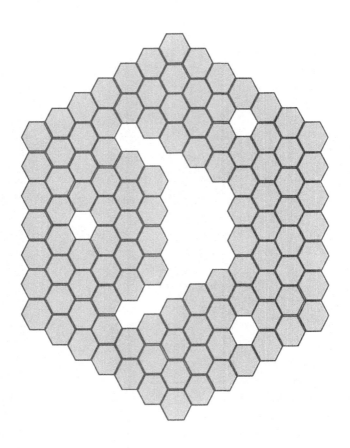

54 – Goddess Moon

Use

the moon

as a portal

to deepen the

conversation

with Goddess.

Honor all the

natural cycles

and rhythms

of life.

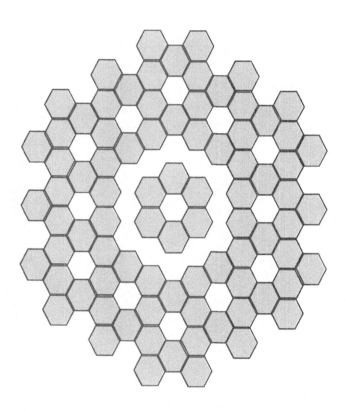

55 - Appreciation

There is no reason to be in judgment of anyone.
There is no reason to exercise any agenda or control.
Being against anyone or anything reinforces that condition.
At this moment, it is time to let go completely of all attempts to
Fix **or** solve   any problems.
Trusting in Divine perfection instead of perspective is the mechanism.
Feeling Self-compassion in every   moment activates the mechanism.
The world isn't what it appears   to   be from a conditional perspective.
When you are in the Heart, you are aware that everything is connected.
Divine Love allows everything to exist in the form it currently exists.
Politics, religion, environment, technology, warlords, and priests.
To bring any   One or thing into harmony with   potential,
you simply   Love them.
Simply BE in Heart   Presence with All.
Turn your attention to the Heart.
Especially Her's.

When you Love what is,   regardless of perspective,
you alchemize potential.
Potential is every One's   most Divine expression.

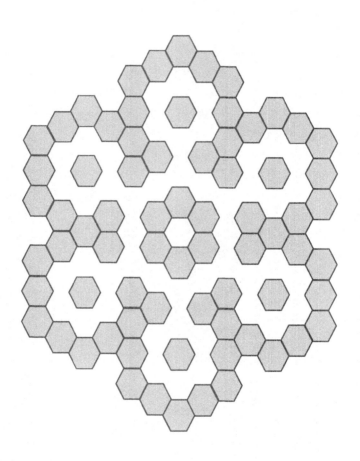

56 - World View

Leaders in
every level of consciousness
are helping to hold each level together in
government, religion, commerce, education, transportation,
security, medical, monetary and communication institutions. It's important to
have leadership in all of those levels.
Judging heats up the pot, adding pressure.
Change under pressure becomes destructive.
Things allowed to evolve, shift gracefully.
All levels are reflections of your human consciousness.
7+ billion centers of the Universe projecting in the mirror.
Every One is exactly where they are required.
Everything is Divinely placed.
It's already all perfect.
So Love what is.
Discard your stories.
Use the mirror to see what to Love.
Keep loving until it is only Love.

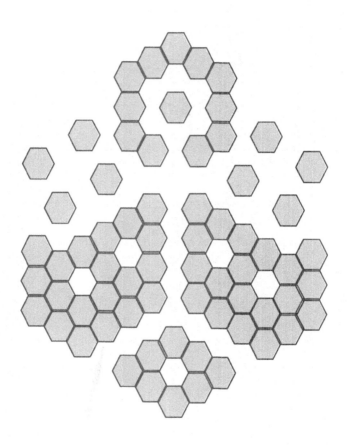

57 - The Environment

It was known long ago that a special place was needed to help souls who had reincarnated many times to work out collected shame and shadow. The design was perfect - Clean rivers and salty oceans to detoxify. The creation of Earth is akin to building a great amusement park. In the beginning everything is shiny and new, but as the park serves it's purpose, there is wear and tear. There is no wrong with what is happening on Earth. It is but a cycle. Remodeling of the entire park is just beginning. Soon everything will return to shiny and new with improve -ments. You cannot heal the Earth by figuring out solutions. The Earth is healing because you are learning to Love your Selves. When the shame is gone and you return to Love, your gratitude becomes the cleansing agent Gaia requires. It is already happening, it is quickening and it is beyond science. Everything is already Love, and everything is made up of exactly the same materials. When you use Heart Language to presence Her, your gratitude harmonizes all atoms back into perfection. And since it's all connected, She evolves easefully before you.

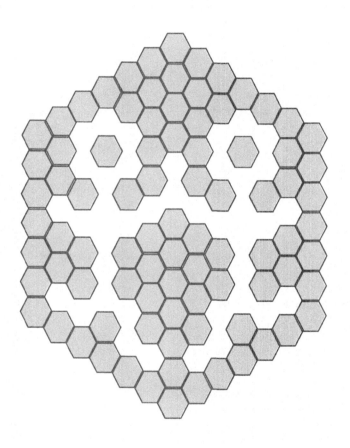

58 - Changing The World

Yes,

In Her

Loving Arms,

The Divine has Earth.

Animals and Humanity too.

So,

Letting go of the feelings and beliefs that support a limited perspective is

all any One can really do to exact change into the world.

Find a way to say Yes for the gratitude of the perfection of Your life.

Be in profound gratitude for every One & thing.

This sends a powerful ripple of potential into the consciousness.

When you choose to see the world as a mirror, use the reflection to heal us

all.

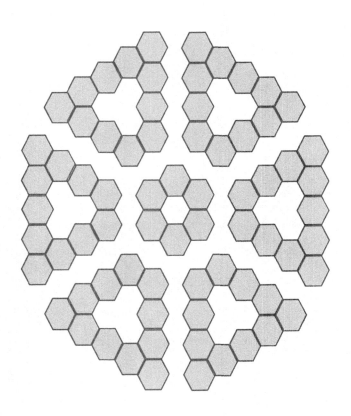

59 - Healing After A Break Up

Find a new way of being in Love with Her.
Send Love to Her with pure intent from your Heart from afar.

Find a new way of being in life.
Free your Self from shame based action and learn to be still.

You have a funny relationship with pain.
You don't want to feel it, so you block it away.
And yet, it is the evolutionary nectar you require for awakening.

Celebrate the resurrection of your Self.
The dying ego comes with you, transformed.
Love the spirit of what you enjoyed with Her,
Rather than tell painful stories.

Remember, your language is creating your now reality.

The great learning within is to take jealousy, bitterness and hatred as a great
opportunity to invite the Divine Love Consciousness to eradicate all illusion of
suffering and return One's Heart to its fullest expression.

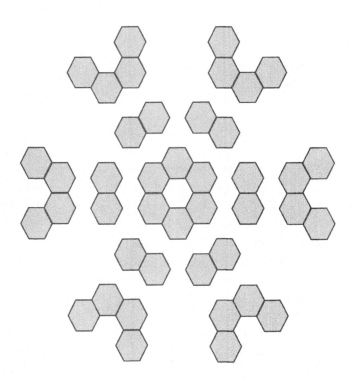

60 - Relationship Endings

Stand for

all relationships ending in Love.

The suffering of a breakup is the unrevealed Truth.

When you are fully revealed in relationship —

then when it ends,

it ends naturally.

Say genuinely:

"May I help you move out into life?"

All humans go through relationships for contrast.

When you can't have someone you truly Love. It's a gift.

Use the gift to awaken your Self to potential.

Something far more expansive.

True Divine Love.

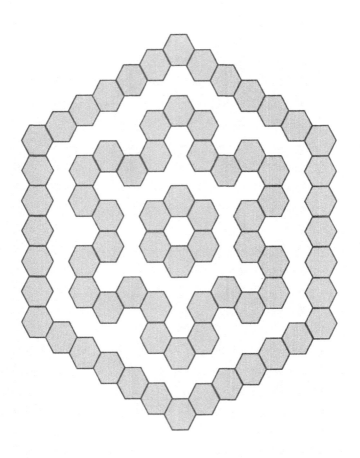

61 - Boundaries

In creating a free world, how does setting boundaries between people you imagine as hurtful, set the example for everyone else?

In un-conditional love, you set the boundaries, but in Divine Love, lines are established by the Heart flowing as natural order.

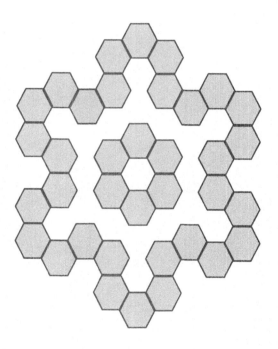

62 - Loving You

Loving your Self
is loving your own medicine -
Loving the totality of your unique expression.

Love Her unique expression as it is - Her medicine.
Because when you Love Her in Her totality,
you do the same for your Self.

When you find fault in another,
you are simply discovering a clue
as to a hidden aspect in yourself
desiring to be loved by you now.
Appreciate this inside aspect.
Surrender into the space
Between   emotion
and story line.

Rapid transformation.

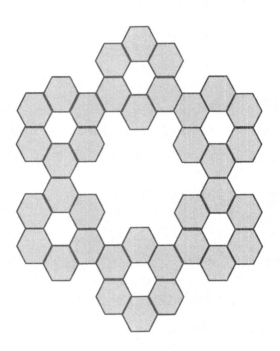

63 - Integrity

How efficiently One uses Heart Presence

to bring forth pure authentic self-expression in One's Self,

and pollinate the One's around You.

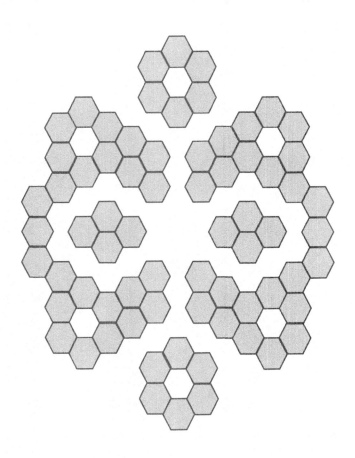

64 – Sexuality

is

shifting.

Sexuality

is

using   sexuality

The Intelligence

and

healing…

for   awakening

rather than

purely for

procreation.

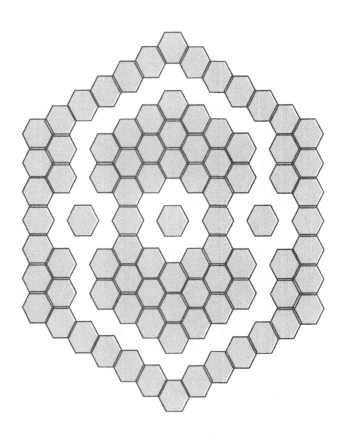

65 - Intercourse

Honor the most Sacred Act.
When you make Love with Her,
She becomes your awakening partner.

You have entered the sacred womb of creation.
You have planted the Holy seeds of Light together.
You have agreed to share both of your sacred medicines.

The moment you experience Her in this way all of life changes.
These seeds sprout first in the form of expanded euphoria and Love.
They later grow into healing opportunities, then into greater Love.

Being in integrity with the Heart is honoring this cycle.
Leaving Her when it gets bumpy is karmic looping.
Adding lovers, invites drama and confusion.

Stabilize your energy field and
Master Heart Presence
with One partner.

before you go looking for more.

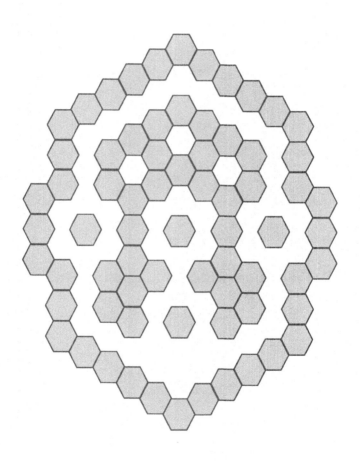

66 - Multiple Sex Partners

Having multiple sex partners and or other sexual releases,
is not a bad thing — it is merely a play of energetics.

Is it expansive? Or something else?

> *Having multiple sex partners*
> *opens multiple circuits of*
> *healing, and therefore the*
> *responsibility to presence*
> *that healing. The illusion of*
> *finding sexual freedom with*
> *more than One, activates*
> *an invisible network for self-*
> *disempowerment rooted in*
> *scarcity consciousness. What*

is rooted in your impulse for more?

To honor two or more Goddesses simultaneously
while in integrity with the Heart is a Wizard's trick indeed.

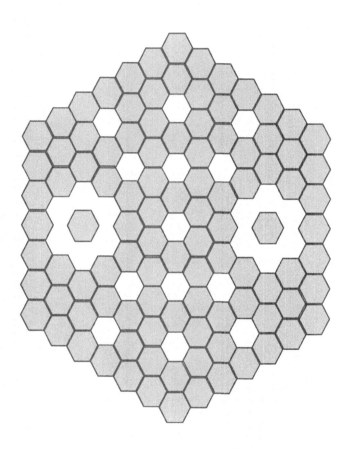

67 - Rejection

. . . .   *How quickly can you take youR*

B   ankruptcy,

H   eartbreak,

Addiction,

Firing &

Anger as

A

Gift

Of Love

From the Goddess?

She invites to own YOU are creating your life.

All aspects brother,

are love.

Gift

It.

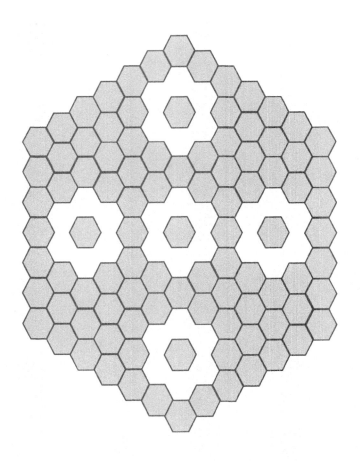

68 - Divorced With Children

Now

separate,

but together.

Find a new way of relationship.
Trust Children are Centers of their Universes.
Honor them as having powerful manifesting powers.
Share your feelings with each of them.
Be very transparent.
Yes.

How can you serve the highest outcome for their lives?
How can you be in the integrity of your Heart and your co-parent?
Create new clear agreements based in the Heart.
Start by being in Love with Her again.
The Love is still there.
Find it.
Yes

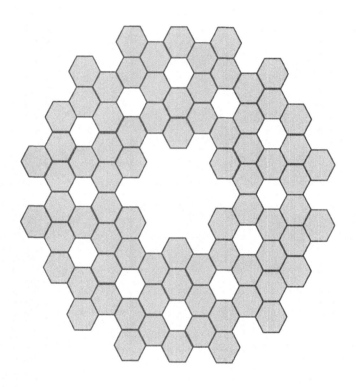

69 - Forgiveness

Return to Innocence.

Until you know,
there is nothing to forgive — Say:

"I am sorry for taking advantage of the Feminine.
Please forgive me, for now I see the Goddess in You.
Thank you for calling me to my soul.
I Love You."

When you have thoughts of regret.
It's simply a reminder to be in forgiveness.
Yes, the moment you notice old feelings and judgment,
open your Heart to find the energy holding the old stories.
Forgive the feeling of the energy,
And return to innocence.

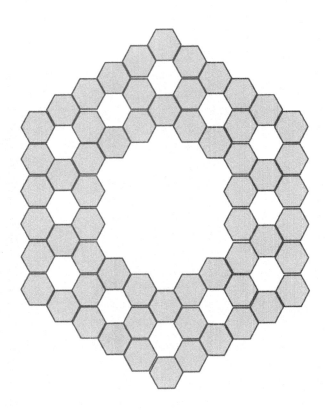

70 - Compassion

H u m i l i t y.

An e x p   *A*   *n s i o n*

of the   *energy*

of the   *Heart*

result-   *ing from*

the recog-   *nition of*

the extra-   *ordinary*

vastness   *of raw*

human-   *ness*

that re-   sides

in every

One.

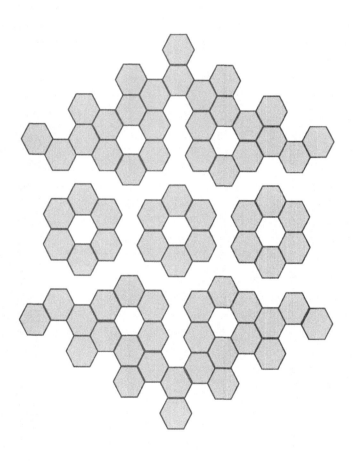

71 - Projection Field

A

field

of projection presents challenges to those on the verge of awakening.

Don't take it personally. It's signaling a huge shift.

You are being tested.

Own Your Truth.

Keep loving.

Keep forgiving.

Keep courageousness.

Spread Your Wings and Fly.

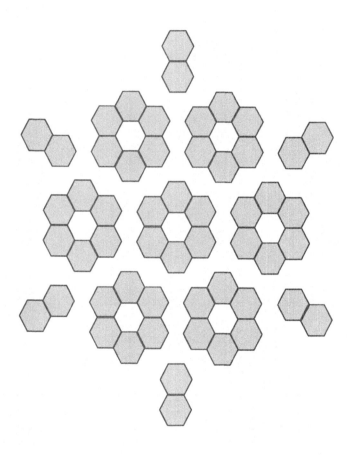

72 - Emergence

When   *you*

         no   *longer*

            care   *for*

              the   *opinions*

               of   *others*

               and   *your*

           *mind resides in the seed space of **Y**our*

                     Heart.

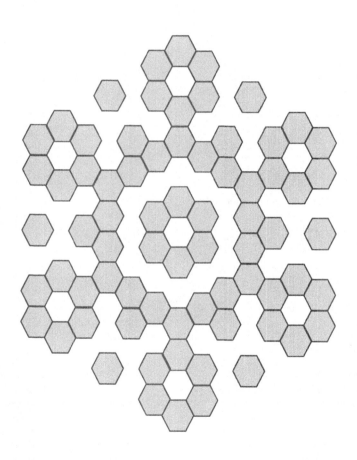

73 - Masculine Desire

A man's needs are irrelevant to the extent of his desire.
Separate your neediness from your life's recipe.
Allow desires to be born from the Heart.
Your higher Self has the blueprint.

Any man attempting to misuse a Woman's Desire
is interrupting the most powerful and natural force in the Universe.
Take your horizontal desire for control and sex, and shift the desire
to Your Heart. This is the beginning of reclaiming your

Divine Masculine Power.

It begins with one simple question:

How May I Serve?

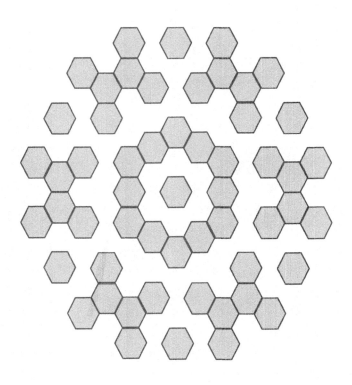

74 - Sexual Attraction

A most courageous action:
Explore sexual attraction without sexual release.

The most courageous attraction:
Allow Her to explore sexual attraction with others.

What is best for Her?
Allow Her to dance freely.
Go slow and keep all Hearts open.
Play the space between attraction and release.
Courageously sharing all feelings in the experience.
Go into experiences to heal sexual shame while honoring desire.
The Absolute Yes is the indicator for every move.
Open the doors to potentiality,
By staying powerfully
in Your Center.

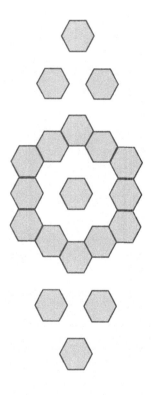

75 - Sitting Still

It is

a natural

process to project

insecurities upon another.

Your role: Guide Her to the other

side of the river in the ferry of your Heart.

There are a million ways to solve your problems.

And none of them arise from opposing The Goddess.

BE willing to be with Her in a way you've never been before.

Appreciate all of Her. In her totality. Every single aspect of Her.

BE the Light.

Invite Her in,

shine the Light.

and honor Her.

BE completely neutral as She reveals herself.

She is just the way She is in this moment.

For you to be dissatisfied,

angry or judgmental. . .

Who the bleep,

are You

?

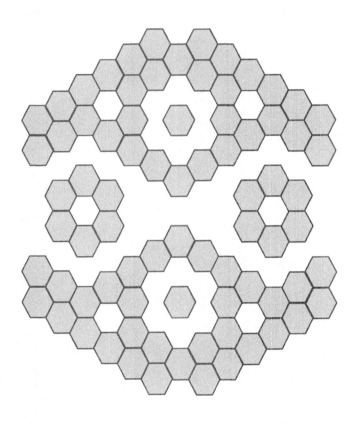

76 - Open Relating

O p e n

every relationship.

Can you find freedom in Love?

Humans are by design open-relaters.

Being in the purity of the energetic connection while honoring the sensual

nature of all our Selves allows for transformation.

Where humanity is going cannot be imagined from here.

Impossible to forecast and discover except through Radical Trust.

A place of having 1 sexual partner and being sensually open in the Heart.

In the meantime, there is no shame in exploring your addictions —

your shadows.

Not from a place of succumbing, or satisfying desires,

but to experience them as great sources of

power which propel you

into awakening.

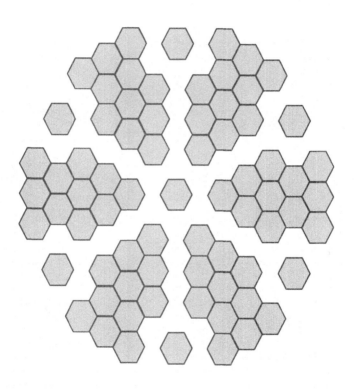

77 - Open Relationships:

She meets someone

who lights Her up in a way impossible for you to match.

This is a Truth.

When you are open to giving Her what She wants, you must meet the madness in you that wants to possess and keep everything the same.

However no-thing ever stays the same.

Co-create higher relating to transcend old paradigms.

Allow all Centers of the Universe to be in free will.

This initiates Her illumination as a Goddess.
The ultimate truth is you are the One.

You can have many loves.
But you are the One.

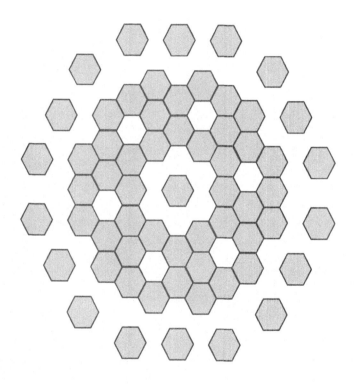

78 - Clear Agreements

Be

This Man.

Honor Her truth.
Nothing is right or wrong.
Be transparent with your feelings.
Agree to communicate in Heart Language.
Agree to find the Absolute Yes in creating agreements.

Agree together to amplify frequency by meeting agreements.

Your mutual individual empowerment is the intent.
Orient your language to the present now.
Co-create reality to meet agreements.
Agree to awaken One another.
Agree to Trust Radically.

Agree to Love

Yes.

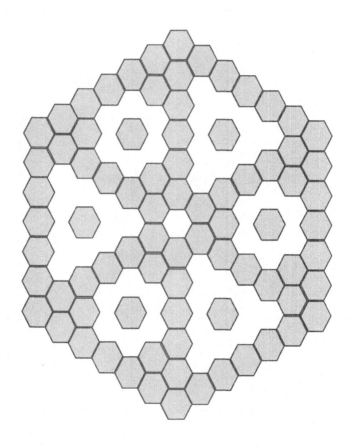

79 - The Triangle

3

is a

Most

Magical

Number. It

is the energy of

transformation. When

your union is challenged by a third party, it is a signal of energy moving.

Invite compassion and transparency so that all triangle aspects

are empowered. Being present with what is happening

without lustfully engaging on the horizontal plane,

gives space for old characters to be revealed,

and for new Pathways of Empowerment to open.

When the triangle opens, It's up to you to be in your

Heart's integrity & your agreements. Being still with the energy

in triangulation utilizes the energy of evolution in an empowering way.

This flips the triangle into

a holographic shape. A

Most Magical

Number

is a

3.

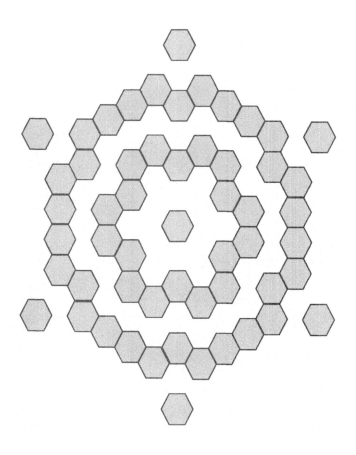

80 - Transparency

The

One

point of activation for your empowerment is

T r a n s p a r e n c y

*With **any** withholding of Truth, you*
create static, disharmonizing your energy field.
You have immediately lost resonance with the Goddess.
She may not know what exactly, but She feels something is off.
Your shared Love state reflects the mutual willingness of transparency.
It's the willingness to go into the fire of your inner angst and reveal your Self.

Own
your Divinity,
As the totality of You.

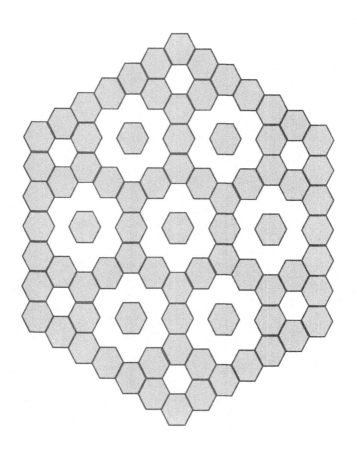

81 - Upgrade Belief

Yes

everything

& every One is evolving.

Therefore every One is awakening.

Therefore every One and everything is healing.

When we allow all Centers of the Universe to be in their

fullest expression, no One is ever right, and no One is ever wrong.

We

Can

All

Get

What

We

All

Want.

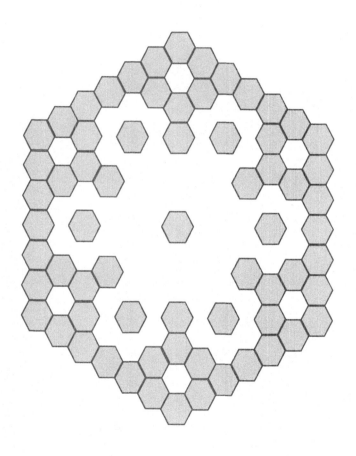

82 - Create More Space

Keeping your pants on but being sexually open allows life contrast.
Use the reflection of contrast to witness story and feel pain.
Notice how your energy wants to move and thrust
horizontally. Breathe in and out of the Tiny
Space in the Center of your Heart.
Focus your will on centering
your awareness in the
Tiny Space.
Ask
for help
in expanding
the Light of the Heart
into the Light of the Universe.
Summon your negative mind thoughts
and relax your gut, allowing energy to move
into the vortex opening in your Heart. Breathe deeply
in the Center of Your Heart. Momentarily hold the breath,
lift your chin, throw back your arms — and then release everything.

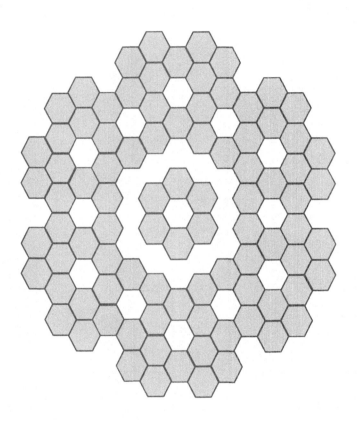

83 - Medicine

Yes,

The   Great

Mother   is   a   flower,

Constantly   blooming   growing,

and pollinating.   She   provides everything One

requires   to   Heal   &   Awaken.   She

provides   essences   and

herbal   remedies for   all

affliction.

How

can

s o m e   t h i n g

be

bad

when

it is a

product

of nature?

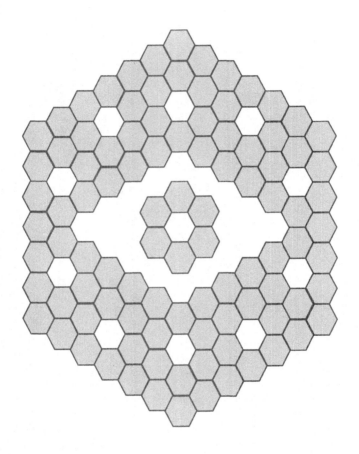

84 – Matchmaker

you are One with your
When   Heart,
You know your vibration is the matchmaker, so
there
is   no
more
looking. The standard you hold for relationship
is ex-.   to you
actly what you attract

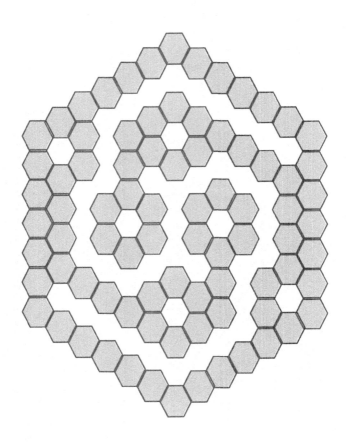

85 - New Relationships

Keeping your pants on was worth it.
When you meet someone in an Absolute Yes,
can you reveal your Self without attaching storyline?
The Universe brings you a Gift. Trust Her.
An opportunity to fall out of story.
She is with you this moment.
BE authentic and real.
Reveal your Heart.
When you Give Her What She Wants there is no reason for her to stay,
except for a pure heart's connection.
But, isn't that what You absolutely want?
Intend relationship that empowers both of You.
Cultivate a mutual Heart Presence free of storylines.
Radiate the Love of your connection to everyone around.
Take this energy to your life purpose and let it serve others.
Appreciate the Gift and amplify your intent for spiritual growth.

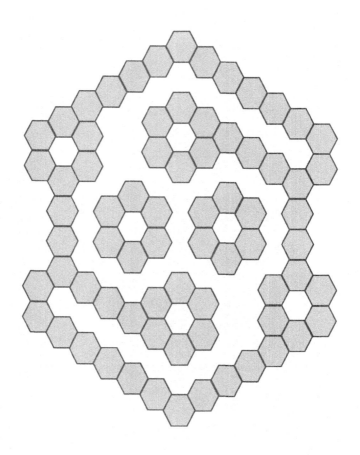

86 - True Intimacy

When you choose to become Her lover,

You agree to take Her medicine.

Fall in Love with your Self

as you fall in Love

with Her.

Yes.

If you are there for your own pleasure, you are polluting Her well.

Cut out expectation and step into a new way of being with Her.

You have a greater capacity for Love than you recognize.

You are a lover - monogamy does not serve you.

At least not the way ego sees monogamy.

Having one lover is powerful,

but to be truly open

to Divine

Love

invites you to be open with all things and people in your Heart.

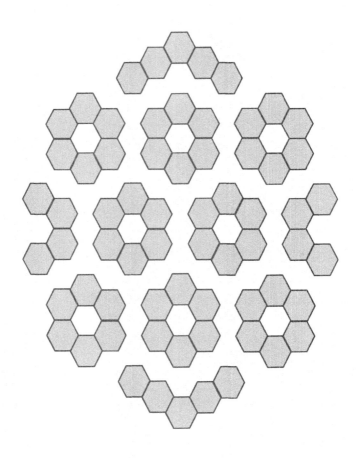

87 - Amplify Frequency

Yes

Your commitment to meeting agreements adds power.

Spend

And, Be fierce to meet your agreements.

time with other

Agree to use Heart Language.

Centers of the Universe.

Agree to use Heart Language.

time with other

And, Be fierce to meet your agreements.

Spend

Your commitment to meeting agreements adds power.

Yes

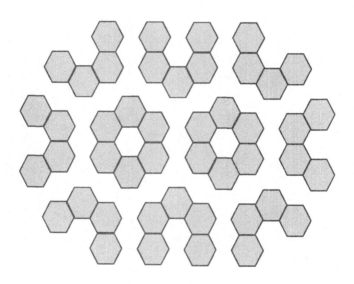

88 - Formulate Your Truth

The

Truth of Yes.

Everyone has Truth.

Write down Your Truth.

Describe Your Heart's Desires.

Create Reality Now in Your Heart.

The alchemy with Her opens the Tiny Space.

From a clear Heart, set your intent.

And follow the Absolute Yes.

Feeling all

Now.

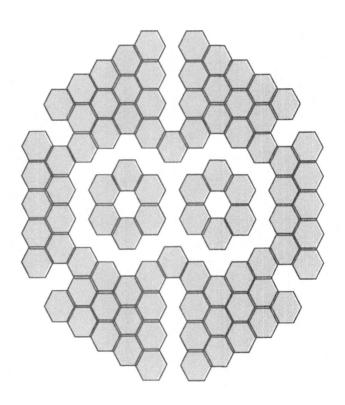

89 – Timelines

*All
storylines
are bound to
time.*

Your new truth is revealed

from the space of nothing in your Heart

*When She is
newly in your
presence,*

*how can you
honor the
fantasies your
mind is dreaming,*

*while
dancing
with what
Love wants?*

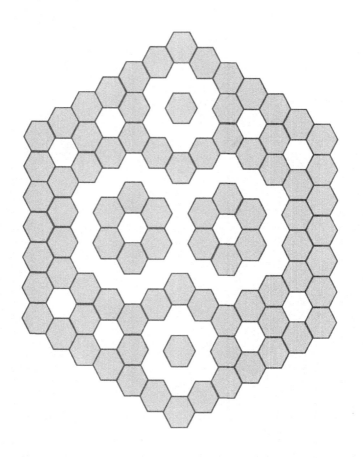

90 – Commit

You

have an

old game called

Poke Her. In this old,

game you move All-In. You commit

all of your gold. One man wins all chips.

All the others are depleted. Now, play a new game.

Move All-In on the Absolute Yes with the Heart's Gold.

Yes, in joy, Give Her Exactly What She Wants. Open

the back of the Heart to the Currency of Love.

Celebrate   playing   a game

where all

cups are flowing,

peacefully together.

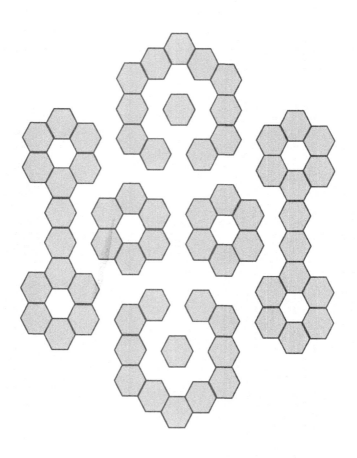

91 – Destiny

Freedom

of

E x p r e s s i o n

You are choosing Destiny in every Moment,
And in every moment, Destiny is choosing You.

Dance between the edges of nothingness,
Allow your Heart to Open
for the birth of a
new One - in
You.

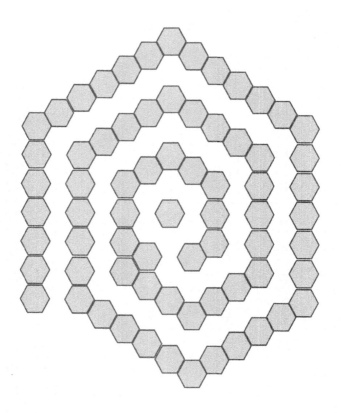

92 - Life Purpose

When a man breaks from the pack for the spiritual journey:

Ridicule.

To continue the journey, he must incinerate:

What is in this for me?

He then encounters fierce opposition.

To continue the journey, he must incinerate:

What can I do to fix problems?

When a man meets Himself in the Heart as the Divine Masculine,

He rests in curiosity,

"How Can I

Serve?"

Healing is initiated.

A path for Self-realization appears.

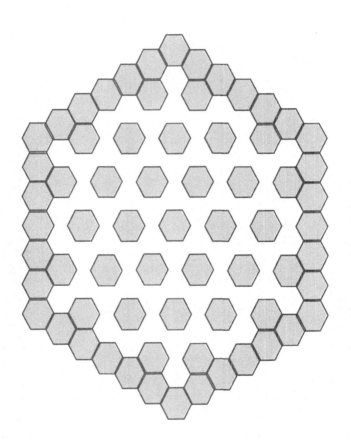

93 – Enthusiasm

Your

enthusiasm is the result of acting on Absolute Yes,

again

and

again.

and

again.

When you are in the Absolute Yes, you are flowing with the Universe.

Enthusiasm

is your

natural

state.

Fly with Dragons to see through illusion.

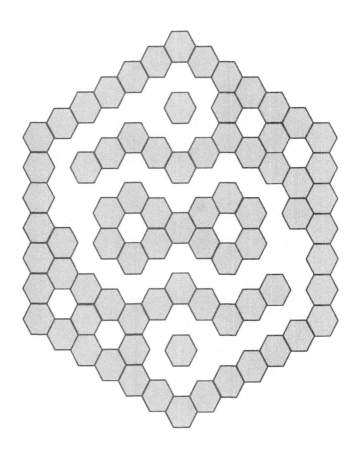

94 – Alchemy

When two
Centers of the
Universe come togethe**R**
in the Absolute Yes.

you say:

"She is the Woman   with whom   I am in alchemy,

I am conscious   of what   my Heart desires.

I am discerning   with   my language.

For in   Her   Presence

desires of the
Heart are always
manifesting."

Yes

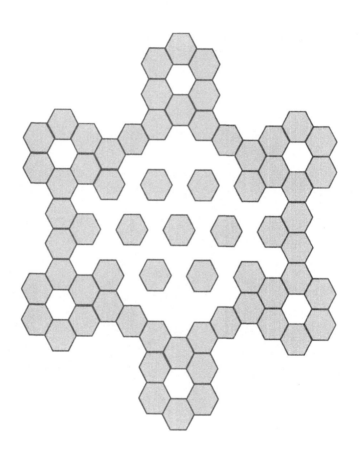

95 – Community

Yes.

Love Rules.

Harmony

is fostered. Anything becomes possible. The Children are healed - in every One

as people communally Heart Presence together, co-creating space

for individuals

to rise into

potential.

A group of people

who's collective Heart Presence

holds no story.

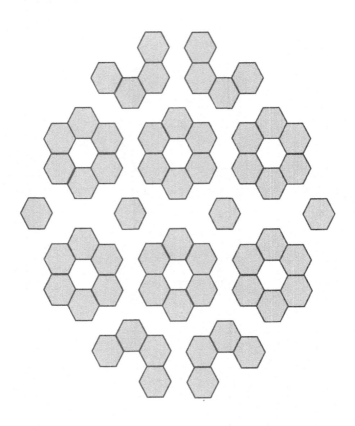

96 - Impact

It is happening.   *Heart Language*
based relationships are so   *magically and amazingly*
transformative, people naturally   *are inspired to live harmoniously*
in proximity, causing compassionate   *fun communities to naturally form.*
Yes, these communities are so attractive, that more and more people join
and extend outward to start new like-Hearted communities. These
"Yes Communities" create enlightened pockets of reality in
societies that quickly grow, invisibly shifting
human consciousness from within,
like transformation of
caterpillars into
butterflies.
Yes.

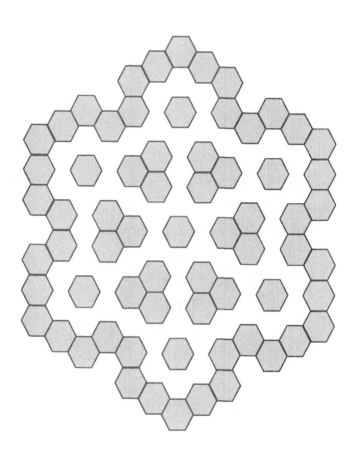

97 – Symbiosis

And   *then,*

When the   *influence*

of your outdated   *language fades,*

And the Heart communities   *connect and merge as One,*

Every One will know what the Goddess already knows,

All is Provided For Now.

We Can All Get What We All Want.

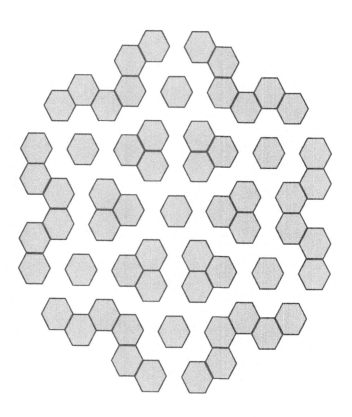

98 - Spiritual Teachers

There is no hierarchy in this new paradigm.
We are all here as mirrors to another.
Open to having many teachers.
Always BE a student.

Teach many to Open.
Be a mirror to others in Love.
Stand in the fullness of your power.
Impossible to elevate a Center of the Universe.

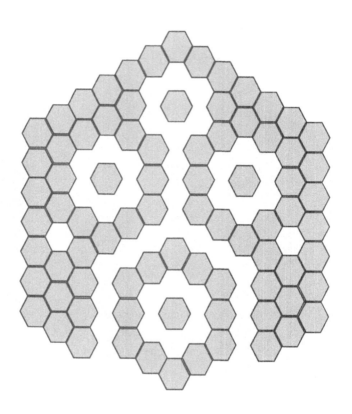

99 - Intuition

Every One has access to Divine Guidance.

An Open Heart is the conduit.

The Goddess is modeling intuition for you.

Pay attention to Her reflection.

Look into the mirror

to see what is.

Be with

that.

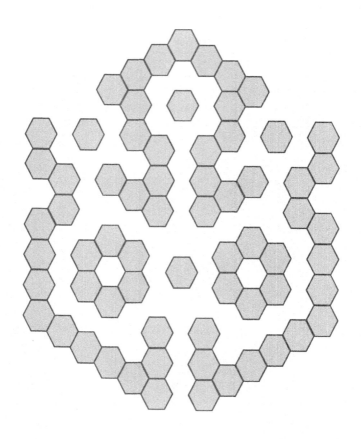

100 - Sacred Sexuality

Yes,

reclaim

the sacred.

To bring ritual to the most Sacred Act is a potent container for

the vehicle of

transformation.

What is possible with your One Sacred Lover is far more expansive were

you to share it with

more than One person.

Be patient with the energy.

Bless Lovemaking with ceremony.

Reveal your Self in the presence of it.

Take the fullness of the medicine of Her.

Use the connection to open to higher truth.

Until the energy no longer invites you both in.

Or takes you higher into an ecstatic state.

Breathing deeply always.

Spread your expanded Love for the benefit of all in your community.

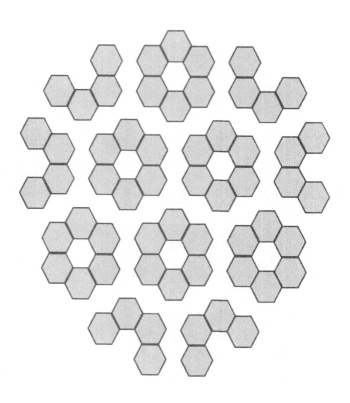

101 - Attraction State

What is coming into your now,
does so because of your vibration.

The wisest and most fortunate men
in the world are surrounded by Goddesses
because they know how to Love them Divinely.

These men have cultivated a higher awareness carefully and stay
dedicated to being in the integrity of their Heart with practice and humility.

These Evolutionary Guides

consciously and continually place themselves completely in their vulnerability
not knowing the outcome until the outcome has come and gone so many times
in so many different ways. In doing so, they allow the forces of spiritual
creativity to burn away all illusion they are separate from the God-
Self residing in the Tiny Space of their ever-expanding Heart.

Keep it chill, keep it tame and Love them all the same.

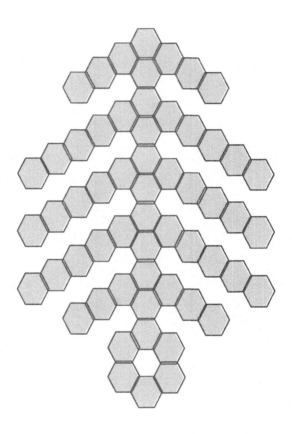

102 - Free Will

In

all-ways

it is your choice:

To Go

with the flow of the Goddess.

Or not.

To Go

with the flow of Mother Earth & Nature.

Or not.

To Go

with the flow of the entire Universe of Creation.

Or not.

Ask the Trees.

Their wisdom guides.

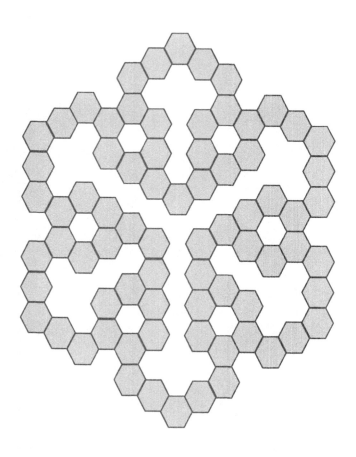

103 - Give It A Way

Everything you desire is already here.
Don't go looking for it.
Give it a Way.
Now.
Give it a Way from within and open to receive.
Your life is all about healing.
Which is to say, the dissolution of all things but the Divine God in you.
Give Her what She wants until there is nothing left but this Truth.
Give Her what She Wants until You are completely empty.
Then give Her more, until the Back of Your Heart is
open and there is nothing but negative space.
Become nothing to obtain everything.
Eradicate the desire to succeed.
There is nothing there.
It is the thrusting that must be softened now.
Become receptive.
It is already here, now.
Align language with the Heart,
And BE very careful what you wish for.

All is Provided For Now.

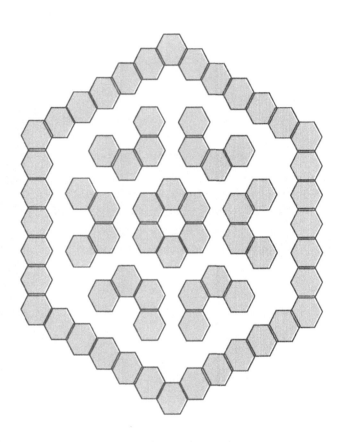

104 – Be The One

When you notice you are thinking She is the One.

Or wanting to find the perfect One for you.

It's a projection of your need for someone to be what you have not embodied.

Mastery is knowing you as the One.

Direct your attention into those things giving you pleasure.

Trust the Heart is Divinely

orchestrating your next

connection perfectly

for you. The

Absolute Yes

happens

now.

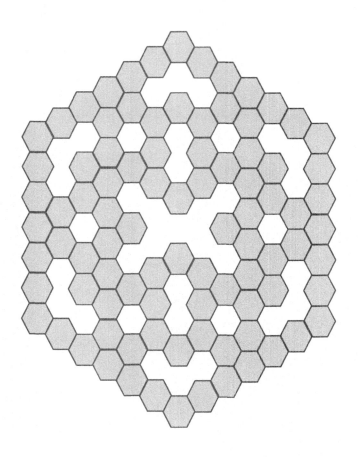

105 - Hall Of Mirrors

When the holographic reflections multiply and become impossible to ignore,

The Universe is demonstrating an expansion of your consciousness.

Keep multiplying, for it is a sign of emergence.

An omen of Divine Orchestration.

Something is happening.

But is it real?

One

can only trust

something isn't destruction

but dissolution of an old construct.

Leave the old ways of relating behind by being still.

Reach out to your closest brothers and become vulnerable and humble.

This is a Now moment to reclaim your sanity & plant your Self in the ground.

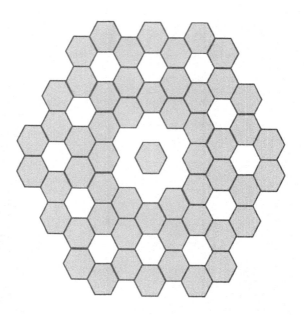

106 - One Truth

Know Your
Truth

The highest integrity of relationship is created from Absolute Twin Yes.
She becomes One you Love, until the mission with Her is over.
It may be 7 minutes, 7 months, 7 years or 7 decades.

Now, stop projecting She is the One.
And become the One for Her.
Yes, You are the One.
It is up to you.
Life is a gift.
Keep on gifting.
Express appreciation.
And then give some more.
Open the back of Your Heart.
And receive the Divine Goddess.

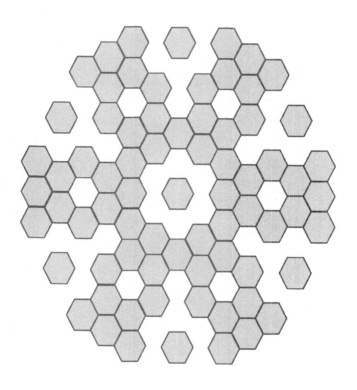

107 - Here IAM

"Here IAM - In a place I wasn't planning to be.
I had just released myself from a field of manipulation and sabotage.
I died a thousand deaths caught in an endless maze of frustration and illusion.

But I stayed committed to my Truth and my work.
And all along while I couldn't see how perfectly it all was happening,
and just when I had recommitted to my Self, the Universe began to present me incredible gifts of relationships and experiences reflecting me honoring my value. It was me all along. Everything was powerfully and perfectly in place for me to receive. And it was my Trust in my Heart that took me through the fire and back to Her. And in that moment I wanted nothing, because in Her eyes is the same fire as mine, and in Her Heart is the same fire as mine. It only took that one glance and the inner wanting to be complete was met. The pull to find Her, and Me in Her was always strong enough to incinerate my lower persona and illuminate my higher Self - And it is worth it, because IAM the One with the One that completes the match of two wholes. I sit here today in the wonder of all the perfection of life and how everything is already provided.
IAM in a receptive flow with the river of my Heart. I am open to Love and I see the perfection of my heartbreaks and being alone until the Universe reveals what I have always desired in my Heart.

Freedom."

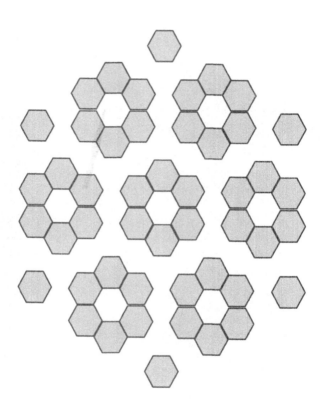

108 - Manifesting

Most
manifestation
is a reflection of your
ego's attraction
state.

When
you think and
act on what you want,
your manifesting is
conditional.

I

I

Listening to Your Heart for what wants to happen and instructions,
opens your awareness to what is already Divinely happening.
Every One and thing is already present for manifestation.
Everything is emerging from your Tiny Heart Space.
This Tiny Space performs like a black hole.
Your Heart draws inward what you feel;
easefully, powerfully, gracefully.
All you have to do, is say: 'Yes.'
Open the back of the Heart.
Go inside the Tiny Space.
Set your Intentions.
Say Yes to Life,
and Bloom.

To initiate manifestation from soul purpose and alignment with your potential
is to utilize a magnetic use of will rather than a reflection of ego.

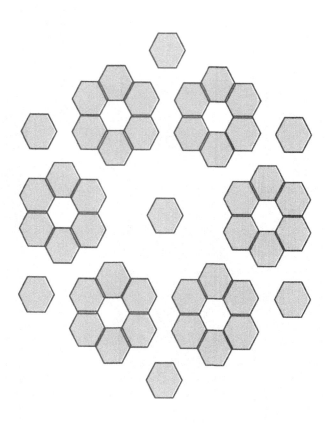

109 - Freedom

Discover Freedom in Love.

Become free in what you dream for

& become free with what shows up in the dream.

Have Radical Trust in the Mystery.

Feel Freedom now to Believe.

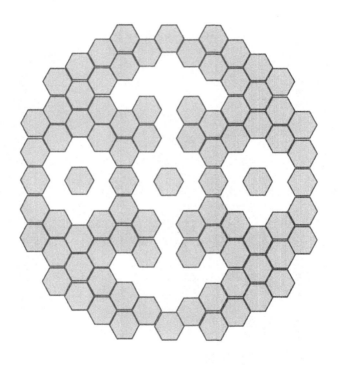

110 - Currency of Love

1 *When the shame is gone, the back of the Heart opens. When the Heart fully opens every One gets what they require to thrive. All is Provided For Now. When the shame is gone, we are one. When the shame is gone, the back of the Heart opens. When the Heart fully opens every One gets what they require to thrive. All is Provided For Now. When the shame is gone, we are one. When the shame is gone, the back of the Heart opens. When the Heart fully opens every One gets what they require to thrive. All is Provided For Now. When the shame is gone, we are One. When the shame is gone, the back of the Heart opens. When the Heart fully opens every One gets what they require to thrive. All is Provided For Now. When the shame is gone, we are one. When the shame is gone, the back of the Heart opens. When the Heart fully opens every One gets what they require to thrive. All is Provided For Now. When the shame is gone, we are One. When the shame is gone, the back of the Heart opens. When the Heart fully opens every One gets what they require to thrive. All is Provided For Now. When the shame is gone, we are one. When the shame is gone, the back of the Heart opens. When the Heart fully opens every One gets what they require to thrive. All is Provided For* 1

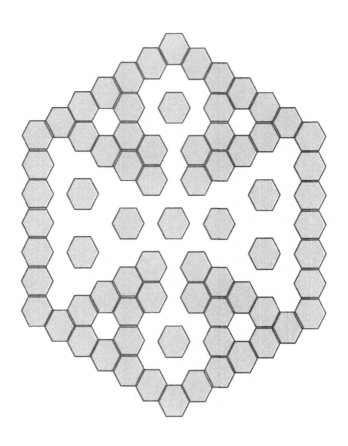

111 - Twin Flame

When She arrives reflecting only

Your Highest Truth

The mirror has no more contrast for you.

Then there is no other.

You have met your Self as the One.

Now all of your creative energy flows into service for All.

Thank you for reading...

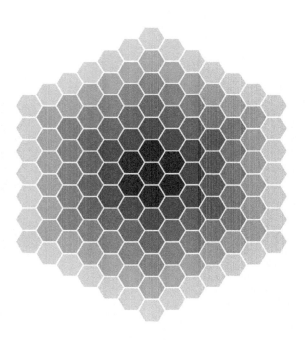

THE GIFT IS
LISTENING

To listen to MysterE read this book,
or visit the River House MysterE School,
please see: www.lifeisheart.com.

Other Books by MysterE:

Your LifeBuilder

ReFrame

The Evolutionary Guidebook

Give Her What She Wants

In Gratitude:

For all the characters and cluster bees who buzz in and out of the
River House MysterE School exhibiting the courage and vulnerability
to be in the freedom of their full expression.

You are the true inspiration.

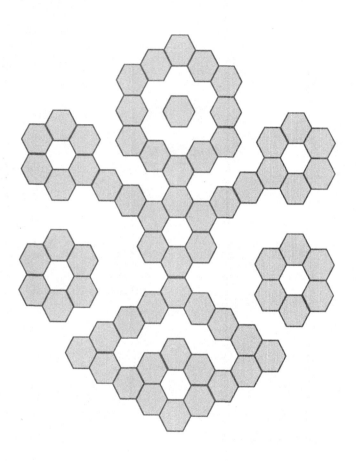